# DEEP in the BRUSH COUNTRY

## LUCILLE THOMAS KRUSE

iUniverse, Inc.
New York   Bloomington

# Deep in the Brush Country

iUniverse books may be ordered through booksellers or by contacting:

iUniverse
1663 Liberty Drive
Bloomington, IN 47403
www.iuniverse.com
1-800-Authors (1-800-288-4677)

Because of the dynamic nature of the Internet, any Web addresses or links contained in this book may have changed since publication and may no longer be valid. The views expressed in this work are solely those of the author and do not necessarily reflect the views of the publisher, and the publisher hereby disclaims any responsibility for them.

ISBN: 978-1-4502-7151-6 (sc)
ISBN: 978-1-4502-7153-0 (dj)
ISBN: 978-1-4502-7152-3 (ebook)

Printed in the United States of America

iUniverse rev. date: 12/02/2010

*To the memory of my parents, John and Annie Mae Thomas and "Auntie," Drusilla Myrick, for filling my life with beautiful memories and to my sister, Catherine Allan, who shares the memories and to my son, John, for keeping the memories alive as he lives in retirement on the old family farm in Falfurrias.*

# PREFACE

For each person there is a place and a time that has molded and nurtured them. After becoming an octogenarian plus eight, the place and time that shaped my life, my values, my choices and my devotions have come even more into focus.

This book is to remember my little hometown of Falfurrias, Texas at the time of its glory and the people who came there to live their dream. And it is to view our little farm home there that flourished with animals, orchards and children. It is also to pay tribute to the dear ones in my family who came to settle in the new land.

For several years I have written articles for my hometown paper, the "Falfurrias Facts." The articles were called "Remembrances." Some of the stories are included in DEEP IN THE BRUSH COUNTRY.

There is a view of what made special occasions, and what "Going Places" was like. Through letters the land is described and advice is given on preparing to live in the new country and what is needed to become a farmer at that time. It tells also of some of the people who had come to this Promised Land and believed it was a great discovery.

It gives glimpses of the older generation looking back to even earlier times and to some of the events that shaped their lives –encountering Indians, crossing an ocean and living in the North Country.

Many of the stories are from the perspective of a child. They show the delights, discoveries and imaginative scenarios that are part of a childhood along with the "Childhood Wisdoms" through which children interpreted their young lives.

But perhaps a realization from the book is the optimism of the time. Life was good and folks thought it probably would get even better. That is one of the gifts my past has given me and that can still be heard in the voices of years ago.

Lucille Thomas Kruse

# CONTENTS

*Rare Sand Verbena, "Heart's Delight"*

*Field of Bluebonnets, Thomas Farm*

# A PLACE CALLED FALFURRIAS

After leaving the Texas hills and rolling country to the north, the earth flattens and the bluest blue sky reaches to the far, low horizons bordered with strips of green. It is the coastal plain of South Texas.

This coastal plain nourishes the growth of hearty trees and brush that flourish in its bed of soft, sandy soil. Here, like the gnarled mesquite tree that grows above the low thorny brush below, the place called Falfurrias has roots that plunge deep in the earth. At times, the mesquite and the earth sleep, baring the thorns of the land that can be so harsh, but then they burst to life—the mesquite with its brilliant, delicate green canopy and the earth with its blazing blanket of flowers.

In its early decades, the people who found the little settlement of Falfurrias and went to live there considered it a great discovery. Flowing artesian water had been tapped, and the desert was blooming. The mood was one of optimism and excitement.

It is said that eons before the time of Falfurrias, the area was submerged under the sea. Then, as the sea receded, it became part of a beach—remnants of which seem to remain with the light, sandy soil that still blows and piles into sand hills.

There was a time when mammoths, giant sloth, camels, and small horses roamed South Texas. Their bones have been found and excavated in and around the creek beds. After the pre-historic mammals came the buffalo, deer, big cats, javelinas, and smaller animals as well as reptiles and birds. Perhaps for millennia the land was theirs alone.

From artifacts of arrows and spear points, we know that American Indians came onto the scene. As their numbers grew in America, some less advanced and less warlike were driven toward the dry desert lands of South Texas. The Indians who came to live inland in the area may have thought

1

of it as a refuge, but without rain, animals and water could be scarce. There was no tall vegetation to use for shelter, so only the very hearty or desperate could survive. They learned which plants to chew for moisture, which to eat for food, and how to be excellent hunters.

From the first shipwrecked Spaniards who arrived in the 1500s, we learned about the South Texas Indians. The Karankawa Tribe on the coast lived mostly on fish and shellfish from the shallow bay waters they traveled in their canoes—made from tree trunks hollowed out by fire. They had small, round houses made of bent poles from willow tree roots. They sharpened the ends of the poles, stuck them in the earth, and covered them with animal skins. The houses could be taken apart, so when they had to move to search for a new source of food, they put the poles and folded skins in the canoes. The Karankawa also made a crude kind of pottery from the clay found in creek beds, and they decorated it with tar that washed up from the gulf.

Away from the gulf waters were the Coahuiltecan Tribes of Indians that were rarely sedentary. They had to be on the move looking for food. Their greatest distinction was their speed and endurance. It is said they could run and chase a deer until it collapsed from exhaustion.

When Texas Territory belonged to Spain and later Mexico, large land grants were given to individuals of Spanish heritage. Some of these landowners lived on their ranches in South Texas even though it was a dangerous and isolated land. They brought cattle and horses and put workers on the ranches. From the heritage of Mexican *vaqueros* (cowboys) who worked cattle with great skill came the practices that are used still today. Stories are told of fierce Indian raids on the ranches that were impossible to defend.

Trails connected the ranches, and to the west through Laredo, the Camino Real connected Mexico with Spanish Forts to the north—San Antonio and Nacogdoches. Travelers crossed the land with their wagons, carts, donkeys, and horses, and they stopped at the ranches for shelter and whatever other protection they offered. The Spanish heritage remains in South Texas with Spanish Land Grant names on the land deeds and abstracts.

After Texas got its independence from Mexico and became a state in the United States in 1846, it was mostly the settlements in the northern part of the state that became more populated. Only after the end of the Civil War in 1865 did a few more settlers go south to what was called the Wild Horse Desert. They perhaps knew of a former riverboat captain, Captain Richard King, who had bought land in the 1850s and created a giant ranch with headquarters on the Santa Gertrudis Creek, which is midway between the Nueces River and the Rio Grande and flows into the nearby Gulf of Mexico. Word spread about the success of his ranch, bringing others who were also eager to acquire land, make a fortune, and create a legacy.

After the Civil War, South Texas was teeming with longhorn cattle, unclaimed and running free. The cattle had descended from those brought in by the Spaniards and Mexicans and those brought in by settlers from the southern United States. The two had interbred and become incredibly hearty. Since South Texas had mild temperatures and was covered in grasslands, the longhorns that could survive on little water thrived. In the famous trail drives, these were the cattle driven up to U.S. railways to be shipped to cities in the north. The area was at the starting point of many of the cattle drives. The longhorn cattle are said to have spread the mesquite trees throughout South Texas and all along the cattle trails. They ate the mesquite beans, and during the three-month drive up to the railways in Kansas, they marked their way with mesquite growth.

Large and small farmers and ranchers came to South Texas in increasing numbers. Fences came in the 1870s. Then railroads came south, and the long trail drives ended. Texas Rangers, with their reputation of fearlessness, came and tamed the countryside. Men ventured into big land purchases with big dreams, great plans, and much daring. The railroad had not yet come to Deep South Texas when in the 1890s, Mr. Ed Lasater came to the area, bought thousands of acres of land, and soon started the little town that he named Falfurrias.

*Henry and Millie Thomas*

# HOW IT BEGAN

People who visited Falfurrias called the area "a Garden Spot in the desert," and I imagine many of the early settlers considered it an oasis as well. The railroad came to Falfurrias in 1904. At that time, it was the end of the San Antonio & Aransas Pass line in Texas. My grandparents, Henry and Millie Thomas, came to live in Falfurrias in 1907 after my grandfather became interested in the promotions of the area that he had read and heard about. He made a train trip to look over the little town and the farmland—and to consider moving. He was favorably impressed with the sandy loam soil that would be so easy to work, the water supply from artesian wells, and the warm climate. He thought the land had great promise. He bought some acreage just west of town on his first trip down from his North Texas ranch near Weatherford. He planned to farm and raise cattle and to collect honey from his bees that he would be bringing. He was confident he could have a great flow of honey considering the tropical vegetation that seemed to be bursting with blooms.

My grandfather, grandmother, and their three teen-age sons settled into the Falfurrias community of about 750 people. The town had a three-room school, two churches (Methodist and Catholic), no brick buildings, and no paved streets. Perhaps since Mr. Ed Lasater, the founder of Falfurrias, and his wife's brothers, Garland, Richard, Lawrence, and Robert Miller, seemed to feel such optimism and enthusiasm for the place, others, too, were caught in the spirit of the time and place and could see great prosperity in the future.

The Thomas family quickly became a part of the lively little town. My father, John, was seventeen when the family moved. He had finished high school and had gone to Weatherford College for one year. He was industrious, highly intelligent, and made friends easily. His first job in Falfurrias was sweeping out the bank at the end of banking hours. He eventually became vice president of the Falfurrias State Bank.

One day in 1915, my mother, Annie Mae Jones, walked into the bank, and my father who was a teller at the time, waited on her. She was a stunning lady with dark hair, soft gray eyes, and a sweet smile. She had the self-confidence of a city person and the gentle warmth of her Southern heritage. She lived with her sister and brother-in-law who had recently moved to town. After she left the bank, John told the other young men at the bank, "Step back, fellows. I saw her first and I want her!" They were married the same year. My father was making fifty dollars a month, and they set up house in their little rented home.

John had grown up on a ranch and wanted to have a home in the country. Annie Mae had grown up in San Antonio and preferred living in town. One Sunday afternoon in 1921, they were riding in their little Ford on a country road a short distance from town. Off the road, tucked among a cluster of trees and vegetation, was a white house with porches and fireplaces. Annie Mae said, "If I could live in a place like that, John, I would like living in the country on a farm." The place was for sale. The next day, John arranged to buy the farm that had seventy-six acres. It belonged to Mrs. Ophelia Collins, whose maiden name had been Fant. She had grown up on the Santa Rosa Ranch (east of Falfurrias near Riviera) that was owned by the Fants. My parents made changes in the house, and part of the remodeling included attaching the kitchen to the dining area. Previously it had been unattached and had a little screened porch passage to the house.

In 1922, I was born on the farm—the third child after John Jr. and Catherine. I was to experience growing up in Falfurrias and would spend twenty years there before getting married.

By 1920, the population of Falfurrias had grown to 2,920 according to census records. In my early years, the town truly looked like a garden. Thanks to the easy water supply, lush vegetation was abundant. Citrus orchards became an industry. The Rupp Family had the largest acreage in the county. Almost every family had citrus trees in their yards. Then the salt cedars (Athal) trees were introduced. My father planted hundreds of feet of them along fence lines. They are a good windbreak and grow into large evergreen trees with thick, heavy branches with soft needle-like leaves.

At some point, cypress trees were brought in. Since they are usually seen in swamps and on riverbanks, it was truly rare and amazing to see them grow big and beautiful in the Falfurrias soil. Palm trees helped give the town its tropical look. There were groves of date palms out in the country and thick hedges of oleanders. Toward the back of our farm, there was acreage of mesquite, and some of the trees were grubbed and cut each year for firewood. It was easy to walk among them; we did not have the underbrush and cactus that grew up in later years. For years we had two mules to pull the plows, and each year "hegira feed" was planted and cut with a "row binder" and then piled into a haystack. The hay was used to help feed the mules and two or three cows that we kept for a supply of milk.

Wildflowers grew in profusion. In springtime, the roadsides were an artist's palette of colors. Bluebonnets blanketed the open fields, and we were especially proud of our radiant and unique flower, the heart's delight. It was said to grow only in and near Falfurrias. It is a rich, lavender, globular cluster of very small flowers (similar to a verbena). It grows close to the ground and has a distinctive leaf and stems that are slightly rough and sticky. We had a bed of heart's delight near our house on the farm. The plants were temperamental; most years they bloomed, but other years they seemed to just wither away or not appear at all. They could be tasty morsels for the rabbits. When St. Augustine grass (carpet grass) was introduced, folks replaced their Bermuda grass, so there were beautiful lawns without the "sticker burrs" and stinging nettles we had before. Our backyard was a mass of periwinkle flowers that bloomed every year—almost out of control.

The dairy business had been promoted by Mr.Lasater, especially with Jersey cattle. Mr. Lasater himself had a prize Jersey herd. (The school athletic teams came to be called Jerseys.) The dairymen sold their cream to the Falfurrias Creamery where Falfurrias Butter was made. For years Mr. Proctor managed the creamery and insisted all cream had to be delivered by a certain early hour or it was refused. He stood on the delivery platform with his watch. He took no chances of having anything other than "sweet" butter. The butter was considered the finest and was shipped nationally. Folks talked of buying it in New York and various places in New England, and it is still being sold today. The town bustled during watermelon season; trucks came in to load from all directions. Trucks were smaller back then; an eighteen-wheeler was unheard of. The little community was largely agricultural with other small support businesses. The one other industry was a gypsum mine south of town. The whole town was prospering.

It was thought by the Falfurrias folks that they had some notable distinctions. The Falfurrias Fourth of July celebration with its parade, barbeque, and rodeo was a great attraction for all of South Texas. And it was with great pride that folks liked to say that Falfurrias was the home of the famous Falfurrias Butter and the beautiful, little heart's delight, a flower like no other.

In the chapters that follow, I will recall the days of growing up on a farm in the little town of Falfurrias in the deep brush country of South Texas, including some of the people and places and the tales of the time.

# "THERE IS A GREAT FUTURE HERE"

Henry Daggett Thomas, my grandfather, was told by his Weatherford, Texas, doctor that he should move to a warmer climate to improve his health. So in 1906, at the age of fifty-three, he began to look for a place to resettle and ranch and farm. He took the train and rode south. He decided Falfurrias was an ideal location. He was a Texan, but he and his family had lived in the Washington Territory for nine years after he had staked a claim near Linden. He had felled huge trees, cleared land, built his own home, and survived two forest fires. A case of red measles left him with hands that shook and a respiratory weakness. He brought his family back to Weatherford, Texas.

In Tennessee, his daughter, Sally, and her husband were thinking of relocating and were considering going to Texas. From letters sent to Sally and her husband, Will Lackey, we gather some information about the Falfurrias area at that time. The following is from a letter dated September 22, 1908:

> *The price of land here that is raw land is all the way from $12 to $75 per acre owing to the distance from town. Just now I know of 40 acres 1 1/2 miles from the depot at $65 per acre. You would have to go 7 or 8 miles from town to get raw land at $12 per acre. The $12 land is on a prairie with practically no clearing to do. The land near town is covered with a thick growth of mesquite and prickly pears. The land is better where the heavy growth is. It is a dark sandy loam—the nicest land to work you ever saw—it would make you laugh after plowing where you have so long.*
>
> *Clearing around here costs from $10 to $15 per acre. That includes grubbing and all. After it is grubbed it plows like old*

*land.*

>*The water is costly $1000 to $1300 to get a flowing well. A well will water 10 to 15 acres of land. Two crops a year. We expect to clear $100 to $200 per acre a year more or less.*
>
>*I like this country. I believe there is a good future for it. People are coming in all the time and some are buying. If it were not for the high price for land and the cost of water it would be filled up right now. Just think of getting Irish potatoes on the market in March. The first ones on the market last March brought five cents per pound. Onions come in April, watermelons in May.*
>
>*I believe you would like this country and I am sure you would have better health here. I think you should come and see us before you settle. I really think it would be to your interest and if you like it I am sure it would be no trouble to locate.*
>
>*You could fix yourself very well for $4000 to $ $6000. One man near me rented his land at $20 per acre and bought it at $80 and has paid it out. He had Irish potatoes and followed with cotton. Now clearing the stalks for a fall crop. He is making money.*

The letter continues and tells about bees and honey that would continue to be a family tradition. Henry was an enthusiastic beekeeper.

>*This is the best bee and honey country I ever saw. It is no trouble to make $10. worth of honey to the colony. If you come here, bring your bees and as many as you can. I brought six colonies and bought four more and we have sold $100 worth of honey and got 23 colonies. I think I will go bigger into the business. They get something the year round and a good honey flow for four months of the year. I have sold all my honey this year for 10 cents per pound here at Falfurrias. If that suits you let me know and I will give you directions how to fix them to ship.*

Sally and Will made the decision to move to Falfurrias. So Henry wrote and gave them some useful information for the move. The following is from a letter written October 20, 1908:

>*We received a letter from Sally today. It seems from her letter that you had decided to come this way. And I thought I would make a few suggestions that I think might be to your interest.*
>
>*Get an emigrant car. And bring everything you can.*

*I got a car and put all our household goods, wagon, buggy, plows, cook stove, six head of horses, cow, chickens, bees and we killed our meat, salted it down in a box and brought it. Millie brought all her fruit. I got free passage and came with the car. Our bees alone have made us enough to pay for the car.*

*It might not pay to bring horses if you can get a good price for them there but it will pay to bring one or two good cows. Butter sells for 35 to 40 cents per pound. Eggs .30 cents per dozen. Coop up your chickens. Fasten the tops and bottoms on your bee hives with long slim wood screws. Tack screen wire over the entrance -- place them where they will get some air and they will be alright -- bring your empty hives and bee fixtures. And if corn is not a good price there slip as much of that in as you can. If you bring some stock the R.R. people will let you put some feed in and are not likely to notice how much is put in. I paid ninety-five cents for some corn today. A good milk cow is worth $75.*

*Bring all the fruit you can. It is high and scarce here. Fruit jars can be packed in sugar barrels. I filled in with cotton seeds. If you can't get cotton seeds hay would do alright.*

*Sally need not bother much about her flowers. Not many that come from the north grow here. This is a great place for flowers and ornamental shrubbery but it has to be adapted to this climate. What we brought with us did no good.*

*The change was alright for our horses and mules .... Bees are worth $4 per colony here.*

Henry, Millie, and their sons became a part of the lively Falfurrias community. Their sons were among other young people who enjoyed picnics under the oak trees, buggy rides down to Salt Lake, and excursions to Riviera Beach. They brought their friends home for visits and Millie's good cooking. Henry was on the school board and was also a county commissioner after Brooks County was created in 1911. He was also a deacon in the Baptist Church. Their son, John, stayed in Falfurrias, worked at the State Bank, and became vice president before establishing his own real estate and cattle loan business.

One son, Robert, lived in Mercedes in the Rio Grande Valley, and the other, Sam, was a soldier in WWI, attended law school, and finally went to live in Houston. After fifteen years in Falfurrias, Sally and Will moved to Taos, New Mexico. The other daughter, Drusilla, came to Falfurrias for a short visit in 1918 and stayed for more than sixty years. She did practical nursing and later was a ladies-wear manager and buyer for the Falfurrias Mercantile Company. When she married Joe Myrick and moved to his farm, she, too, became a beekeeper. She and her father worked the bees side by side. At age eighty-eight and widowed, she built a house in town and lived on in Falfurrias until she was ninety-five years old. She then moved to live with her niece, Catherine Allan, in Austin, Texas.

The land that had promised such a prosperous future failed at times. There were droughts, floods, and freezes. Perhaps the greatest blow for Henry was losing an entire herd of cattle to tick fever. But he showed no regrets for having come to South Texas. In fact, he and his son John often talked about all the opportunities in Falfurrias just waiting to be discovered!

This article first appeared in the *South Texas Historical Association Journal of South Texas*, Volume 12, Number 1, 1999:

*"After the Hunt"*

*Falfurrias, TX l910*

*Park Hotel*

*Falfurrias Public School*

*Group gathered at Salt Lake*

# SPECIAL TIMES AND PLACES

Falfurrias, in its beginning days, was vibrant with young people in their teens and twenties. They seemed to find their new home exciting, full of fascinating people and places. Maybe they, too, were filled with the enthusiasm like that of the founders of their little town. The old pictures and stories of the early days in Falfurrias portray the places—usually outdoors—where young folks went for their picnics and gatherings. The ladies, who always looked slim, wore light colored, long dresses with high necks, long sleeves, and beautiful broad-brimmed hats. They looked like they just walked out of church even though they were at picnics in the countryside. The men, too, were dressed in their best; they wore suits, ties, and hats.

One of the places that seemed special was Salt Lake south of town. Old pictures show that numbers of couples in horse-drawn buggies gathered there. The folks roamed the shores of the lake and climbed the cliffs— including the women in the long flowing dresses! They had picnics under the oak trees, sometimes sitting at tables and sometimes sitting on the ground—but always so dressed up! The shade of the oak trees seemed to be a special attraction.

Huge earthen tanks filled with water as the windmills pumped; they were the swimming pools of the day. Pictures of lady swimmers show bathing suits covering them to the knees. Folks also enjoyed paddling rowboats around on the enormous tanks.

There were few cars in the early days, and those who had them shared rides with friends and took pictures of the occasions. One special trip was the drive east from Falfurrias to Riviera (on a very early paved road), followed by a train ride to Riviera Beach. A narrow-gauge train track had been built by the owner of the large hotel on the Riviera Beach waterfront.

Some folks swam, and others just enjoyed the lovely park and the big hotel.

Many of the men in South Texas were hunters. If someone wanted to hunt deer, turkey, or birds, he just asked a friend who owned land (or a friend might invite him). Friends seemed happy to say, "Bring your gun and come on out." People rarely charged for the privilege of hunting. Some of the most exaggerated stories of the time were probably hunting stories—two dead bucks found with tangled horns, Mexican lions stalking hunters, killing multiple turkeys in one shot, and killing enormous rattlesnakes by the score.

In the earlier days and when I was a child, there were men, including Uncle Joe, who liked to "wolf" hunt with hound dogs. They were actually hunting coyotes and sometimes bobcats. The hunters seemed to like moonlit nights. They would arrange to meet at a certain time and place, usually a location with trees and brush. They would each bring their hound dogs, and then all the men would let their dogs out of their trucks at about the same time. If a hound dog chased a rabbit, he was a big embarrassment and severely scolded. The dogs usually picked up a coyote scent and then charged in one direction, the entire pack sniffing all the way. Our family sometimes saw the hunters when we were coming home from visiting friends in the evening. We would stop and talk to them, but only in whispers. The men were listening to the barking, yapping, baying, and howling of the hounds. Each hunter wanted one of *his* dogs to be the lead dog, meaning that dog was the best. All the men claimed to know the sounds of their own dogs, and often more than one of the hunters claimed that *his* dog was in the lead. The sounds from the hounds changed as they got near their prey, and when they had the coyote surrounded, they attacked and killed. The hunters knew what was happening just by listening. Eventually the hounds would come back to the trucks, though very slowly. They were tired, bloody, and sometimes badly wounded, but they wagged their tails when the men showed appreciation with a firm pat on the shoulder. If one of his hounds lagged or did not appear after the hunt, Uncle Joe blew his horn made from a long curved cow horn. It was a signal they understood to let them know where he was. Maybe the hunters felt some pride in thinking they had rid the countryside of a menace—a coyote that ate chickens and watermelons.

Once in a while, play directors came to town and chose a play to present to the community. They used the town people as the actors, and the high school auditorium was filled for the production. When I was four years old, I was chosen for a one-line part. In the play, I was picked up and whisked off the stage. I suspect I got the part because I was small enough to be carried easily.

For my parents, Rotary Ann night was a special occasion. It was an evening when the Rotary Club members (all men) invited their wives for dinner and entertainment. The master of ceremonies was usually Dick McIntyre, an amusing businessman with a gas station, lumberyard, and restaurant. He told great jokes with dry wit and easy humor. Miss Beatrice Story was a Falfurrias violinist and often entertained during those evenings. The one requirement was that she play "The Flight of the Bumblebee." Folks marveled at her amazing skill as her bow and fingers fluttered over the violin strings.

Rotary Ann night was sometimes an area-wide event, and folks loved to have it at the Case Ricardo Hotel in Kingsville. It was an elegant hotel with a spacious dining area, a ballroom, and sweeping verandas. The lobby had a high ceiling with stained-glass windows toward the top. As with most public buildings of the time, cuspidors were scattered around. Those at the Casa Ricardo were shiny brass. Large outside gardens were filled with tropical vegetation.

My mother was always beautiful with her white hair and smiling gray eyes, but for special occasions she sparkled in her carefully chosen earrings, necklace, and very best dress. My father always showed his admiration for his little "Momasita" when she was "dolled up." In fact, he showed his devotion consistently, and she always returned it with her sweet smile. A single fresh pink rose sat in a bud vase on our dining table every day. Almost every morning, he would pick a rose from our hearty rose bush that bloomed year round and give it to Mother as she lingered over her morning coffee. She was truly a "Little Mother." I never knew her to weigh as much as a hundred pounds. She stayed a very tiny person all of her ninety-one years.

There came a time when Baptist pastors no longer opposed people in their congregations playing cards, so my parents and their church friends gathered often to play canasta. There was big competition and ongoing scores with plenty of playful banter.

During birthday parties for young children of my generation, we played games such as "drop the handkerchief," "tag," "jump rope," and "statue." Most games were running games. There was one pretty birthday cake, home baked and home decorated, if decorated at all. Each child had a piece of cake and sometimes ice cream, homemade by using chipped chunk ice packed in a hand-turned freezer. Cupcakes came in later years. The birthday cake had tiny tokens in it, and getting a token in your piece of cake meant a prediction of your future. A ring indicated the person would get married. A thimble indicated a person would be an old maid (what about the boys?). A coin suggested a person would be rich.

We children loved the Sunday comics that didn't come until Monday because our paper was the *San Antonio Express* and had to be mailed. We pounced on "the funny papers" when they came and spread them on the floor to read. Little Orphan Annie, Mutt and Jeff, Dick Tracy, Popeye (we loved Wimpy), and Terry and the Pirates were some of our favorites. Later, I loved Brenda Starr and truly fell in love with her hero boyfriend (The Mystery Man) who had a patch on one eye.

Parties with young church people came later. We played games like "musical chairs" and "spin the bottle" and had scavenger hunts. For scavenger hunts, each team had a list of objects to find. Lists might include a bird's nest, moss from the tank, cobwebs, or hair from a cat. The team that first found everything on the list was the winner. There were also nighttime hayrides in a hay-covered bed of a farmer's truck. Kids piled in and rode along singing Falfurrias Jersey songs and anything else that was suggested.

When people my age were in their teen years, cars were available, telephones were on the walls, and electricity had come, providing radios with interesting stories and music and news. *Lum and Abner* and *Amos and Andy* were two of our favorite programs. Also, we would gather at a popular place called Oak Grove, which was nestled in a cluster of oak trees south of town. The café there was called Mother's Café, and it had a nickelodean and a floor big enough for dancing. We danced to "Summit Ridge Drive," "Begin the Beguine," "Stardust," "Smoke Gets in Your Eyes," the "Beer Barrel Polka," and other songs of the time. Parents did not always sanction the trips, but Oak Grove was just ten miles down the road and we usually went in the afternoons.

There was one theater, the Pioneer, with at least two different movies each week (we called them "picture shows.") Teens usually went on Saturday evenings, and then after the movie, we went to the White Spot Drive-in for a soda. If a girl was fortunate enough to be dating a fellow with a job, she might also get a hamburger. White Spot orders were taken by a "car-hop" and then brought to the car on a tray that hooked onto the side of the car door. Another after-the-movie favorite was finding a jackrabbit on a country road and seeing whether the car could outrun him. The rabbit usually won and then darted into the brush.

In the 1920s and 1930s, driver's education and driving tests didn't exist. At age sixteen, a person could apply for and get a license, but he or she had probably been driving for as long as they could see over the steering wheel. They had been taught at home by older brothers, sisters, or friends.

There were lots of country roads to learn on, and often it was just a matter of staying in the ruts.

The sand hills south of town were great fun. The sand was beautifully white and fine. We climbed, slid, and rolled over and over on the hills and then later built a fire and roasted wieners and marshmallows, usually in the moonlight. At the sand hills, the girls wore slacks, but they wouldn't even consider wearing slacks to school.

My very favorite place was the Moss Tree. Los Olmos Creek ran just south of my aunt and uncle's farm in a pasture they leased. In our family, it was Uncle Joe Myrick who first saw the Moss Tree. He told us about it, and then he and my aunt walked with my brother, my sister, and me to see it. We worked our way through the brush, and when we finally turned toward the creek, the beautiful tree seemed to tower right above us. It was an elm tree with great spreading branches and long heavy moss draping down and swaying. Some smaller moss trees, too, lined the banks of the Los Olmos. The place was truly magical. We sat in the shade and realized we had found a treasure. On many Saturdays, friends and I rode horses to my aunt and uncle's farm and then hiked to the Moss Tree where we ate the lunches we had packed under the giant tree. When we carved our initials on the trunk, we found weathered carvings from many others before us. The enchanted place was no longer just our secret. Water usually pooled in lower parts of the creek, and birds loved the place as much as we did. I saw my first painted bunting and my first green jay there. The moss tree was so very remarkable and dear to me that I took my husband and two young sons to see it years later. They, too, thought it was a most special place.

# THE FOUR OF US

Of the four children of John and Annie Mae Thomas, John Clyde Jr. was the firstborn—in 1916. Lots of relatives nurtured and pampered him, including his Thomas grandparents, the Lackey family with their grown children cousins, and two bachelor uncles. There are pictures of John Jr. on a horse alongside his uncles and others pictured him in the arms of his cousins. He wore short pants and long stockings in most of the photos. He became my big brother, "Jr."

Less than two years after John was born, Catherine Mae was born. At that time, our father sent for his practical nurse sister, Drusilla, to come and help with the new baby. Our beloved "Auntie" had come into our lives. The plan was for her to come for a few months, but she stayed on in Falfurrias for more than sixty years. Catherine came to call her "Auntie Mother." One of Auntie's concerns for Catherine was that she had so little hair, so she rubbed olive oil into Catherine's scalp every day. Catherine grew thick, silky hair that has never shown any hint of thinning. She was called "Sister Girl," which became "Sis."

Four years later, in 1922, I, Lucille Thomas, was born. My parents did not give me a middle name, and I later wondered why. I went ahead and gave myself a middle name, changing it whenever I came across an appealing new one. Dorothy was a favorite, as was Virginia. Auntie had nicknames for all three of us children, and I came to be "Pet." I am told it probably evolved from "Peaches" to "Petty" to "Pet." Catherine remembers that on the day I was born, she and John were staying with our friends, the Bennetts. The Bennetts were making pink homemade ice cream in their hand freezer when our father came to pick them up to go see their new baby sister. Catherine remembers her terrible disappointment that she had to leave without having any pink ice cream. When she got home, I was sleeping. She looked into my crib and said, "Daddy made me come to see her, but she's dead."

In 1924, Henry Drew was born. He came to be called "Sonny." He was a beautiful golden-haired child with a happy, playful smile. Since John and Catherine were close in age, they were buddies and spent a lot of time together exploring the farm and acting out their make-believe lives. Sonny and I were close in age, so we were close pals for his short years. Sonny died shortly after he turned three years old. After a September morning of playing outside, he took a nap and woke up with convulsions. His fever soared. We had two doctors in town but no hospital. Both doctors came out to the house, and everyone prayed fervent prayers pleading for his life, but he died two days later.

There was a gripping sadness that fell on us; our sweet little brother was gone. His little highchair stood empty, a constant reminder of how he used to eat his supper and then lay his head on the tray and fall asleep.

I spent more and more time outside. I loved climbing trees and being with my dog and later riding our horse. Catherine spent time helping Mother with the cooking; the two of them were like a team. Catherine seemed to know how to lift Mother's spirits, and she also had a special talent for cooking. She found just the right seasonings and combinations and always used generous amounts of cream and butter. My kitchen contribution was making the butter. After about three days of saving cream skimmed off the top of milk from our cows, I would have enough cream to put in the churn and make butter. I liked turning the handle of the churn and watching the cream splash in the glass churn and finally turn yellow and completely separated from the white milk. I poured the milk into a container to be fed to the chickens. Then I put the yellow butter into a bowl and pressed down with a paddle to work out any droplets of the milk. Finally, I put it into a mold or small bowl to use later on the table. At meals, the butter was always in a large, full container, and we used it freely. We had never heard of cholesterol.

When Catherine was quite a young child, she and Mother went with Auntie to San Antonio on a buying trip for the Mercantile Store in Falfurrias. They were eating at the Menger Hotel, and Catherine let it be known that she wanted butter. The waiter brought a plate with small pats of butter, and Catherine threw the butter on the floor. The waiter brought another plate with pats of butter, and Catherine proceeded to throw it on the floor again. Someone finally asked the waiter if he could bring a large chunk of butter. When he did, Catherine was then satisfied with what she considered to be *real* butter.

Jack Dempsey and Charles Lindbergh were John Jr.'s heroes in his young years. He read everything he could about the heavyweight fighter and the famous aviator. He loved to play the card game called "Lindy." John Jr. also had 4-H projects in his teen years. He raised chickens one year and rabbits another year. What became of the rabbits was a mystery. We didn't eat them because it would have seemed barbaric. They were so pretty, gentle, and friendly.

We had a phonograph that had to be wound with a crank. The records that played on the turntable were big and heavy. One of our favorites was of Caruso, the singer, and we also had a record of Amos and Andy that we liked and quoted and laughed with every time it was played. We children entertained the adults sometimes. John told jokes, Catherine recited poems, and I did acrobatics.

Life on the farm helped shape our young lives. Whenever one of the animals had offspring, it delighted us. We also loved to watch and admire the seasonal vegetation. We were especially proud of the citrus, and we children helped gather the fruit. The abundance of fruit harvested kept our friends and relatives well supplied. The long, screened porch was shady and cool in the afternoons, and I found it to be the perfect place to read the Bobbsey Twin books, or fairy tales which I loved.

On cold winter evenings, the whole family clustered around the living room fireplace and tossed pecan shells into the fire as we cracked and ate the nuts. All of us hated to leave the warm fire and go to our cold bedrooms. But finally we did dash into our beds—sometimes with a hot water bottle for our feet. From the bed Catherine and I shared, I could see the few dying embers in the fireplace even after our father had "banked" the coals with ashes.

Catherine and John were good students. They were both salutatorians of their graduating classes, and they both went to college on scholarships. John was a handsome and popular young man who could always see the funny side of life. Catherine was beautiful with perfect skin, lots of lustrous hair, and a keen eye for fashionable clothes, many of which she sewed herself. She made friends easily, and they remained close throughout their lives. I was fourth in my graduation class and more carefree than Catherine, although she was my model.

After we three adult children married and left home, we made "coming home" visits. John Jr. did not have children, but he came with his dogs, and the dogs enjoyed romping in the open spaces. Catherine and I had children that loved coming to the farm where we all gathered on holidays. The cousins played together, picked the fruit, visited the tank, slid down the haystacks, and tried to ride baby calves—just as their mothers before them had.

*Annie Mae Jones Thomas*

*John C Thomas*

*John Jr., Lucille and Catherine Thomas*

*Henry and Lucille Thomas*

*Mr. Ed Rachal*

# REMEMBERING MR. ED RACHAL

For children growing up in Falfurrias during the 1920s and 1930s, "Mr. Ed" Rachal was a special person. He loved entertaining folks, especially children. Our family was fortunate to have him and his wife as our near neighbors.

When I was young, it seemed that having a home on a small farm near town was a way of life in Falfurrias, even though the owners of these small places often had ranches or businesses in town. The farm acreages had citrus orchards, a windmill, an earthen stock tank, a few cows, a horse or two, sometimes mules, small flocks of chickens, and gardens and crops of various kinds. Mr. Ed and his wife Louise lived two farms from our home.

Before I was old enough to walk to the Rachal place, my mother took my brother, John, my sister, Catherine, and me to swim in the Rachal tank during summer afternoons. Children from all over town gathered there, so there was a lot of friendly splashing and squealing. In the background, we could hear the gentle rhythm of the windmill pumping in fresh water. Our mothers sat on the bank of the tank and visited in the shade of the trees. Every few minutes, our mother would call out, "It's over your head in the middle."

Another attraction at the Rachal place was the horses. When I was old enough to ride our horse, I sometimes had friends visiting who did not have their own horse. We would simply walk down to Mr. Ed's, and he would let us borrow one of his. His farm helper would saddle the horse for us, and we were allowed to use any horse Mr. Ed had—except "Upset." Upset was Mr. Ed's prize horse, the only horse that had ever beaten "Man of War," who was a celebrity horse at the time. We children did not really know who Man of War was, but we did understand that Upset was very special and very fast. We would look at him and marvel at his size and greatness and then try to get his attention with little bunches of grass.

Mr. Ed had special talents that he loved to use when performing and entertaining folks. He could do rope tricks, twirling a rope up and down and jumping inside and back. He could sing old Western songs, and he called square dances and quadrilles done on horseback. He performed on stage at special occasions.

In Falfurrias, it was traditional to have a big July Fourth celebration that included a parade, a barbeque, and a rodeo. Mr. Ed led every parade I can remember, riding his horse and carrying the American flag. Our sheriff, usually Jesse Grimes, rode next carrying the Texas flag. Then came Mr. Ed's sister, Mrs. Hart Mussey of Kingsville. She rode sidesaddle and wore a long, flowing, white riding suit.

Mr. Ed's mother lived just around the corner from him with his brother Frank. She was an impressive figure when she sat on the rocking chair on the front porch. She had lots of snow-white hair and wore long dresses, and she told interesting stories about the earlier days in South Texas. The early Rachals had lived at White Point near Corpus Christi, and she told of gatherings at their home where dancing lasted all night long. She also told of carriage trips she had made to Mexico and how firearms were kept ready for protection against bandits. Mr. Ed's father, Nute Rachal, is credited with planting the first citrus orchard in Falfurrias.

On the porches (my Uncle Joe Myrick called them galleries) and on the lawns in the cool South Texas summer evenings, folks would recount a well-known story about Mr. Ed. Years before when Falfurrias was quite young, an Hispanic man had been shot by an Anglo. The Hispanic community was enraged, and a crowd armed with guns came into town for revenge. The Anglo community responded by arming themselves as well, and then they stood on one side of the main street while the Hispanics stood on the other side. Mr. Ed, on his horse, rode in the center of the street, speaking in Spanish and then in English. He rode back and forth, talking to each side, pleading for an end to the violence. Gradually, he persuaded them, and people from both sides left.

One day, a friend, my dog Fluffy, and I were walking by a neighbor's place when a huge German shepherd raced out, grabbed Fluffy in his powerful jaws, lifted her high up, and shook her. I screamed, and Fluffy yelped. The Shepherd dropped her, and I fell over her to protect her, leaving myself at the mercy of the large animal. Mr. Ed was driving by; he saw the situation, rushed out of his car, and chased the big dog away. He rescued my little dog and me! For years after, whenever I saw him, he asked about my little dog.

Mr. Ed's wife, Mrs. Louise Rachal, helped our little town with her promotion of literary and performance groups and her focus on helping children. Among our neighboring families with children there were the Dales, the Words, the Taylors with their grandchildren in the summer, and the Bests who had a son named Nat. We rode horses together—kind of a country kid posse. Nat was black, and under the law at that time, he was unable to attend public schools. So Mrs. Rachal taught him. When the rest of us would talk about school and teachers, Nat would say, "I go to the Rachal School." Nat stayed in Falfurrias, grew up to own his own business, married a schoolteacher, and had a son who graduated from West Point where he was captain of the track team. The son made the army his career and finished his duty with an assignment at the Pentagon.

During a period of time when my brother and sister were in high school, Mrs. Rachal's niece and nephew lived with them. The children had lost their mother and so for a time made their home with the Rachals. They rode to school with us and quickly found their place in the local social life of the young people. Our newspaper, the *Falfurrias Facts*, had an article about a party the Rachals gave for them that included dinner, games, and dancing on the veranda.

When I picture Mr. Ed , I see a slight man with blue sparkling eyes, a somewhat crinkled face, lots of gray hair, and gray eyebrows that were rarely trimmed. His hat was usually pushed to the back of his head, and he tipped it whenever he met a lady on the street, removing it if he lingered in her presence. He and my father, John Thomas, received many compliments on their gracious manners. Mr. Ed always walked quickly and seemed to be in a big hurry. He was a rancher, and when he talked about his ranching, he often told a sad story: "Beef prices are low, and there has been so little rain!" Fortunately for him, oil was found on his dry ranch land. I was never aware of the money changing the way he lived, but it made it possible for him to help the community he lived in.

Much of Mr. Ed's legacy can be seen in his contributions to the lives of children and young adults. He and his wife, Louise, did not have children of their own but were dedicated to enriching the lives of young people. Funding from the Ed Rachal Foundation went to building the Rachal Library and the swimming pool in Falfurrias, and hundreds of college students from Brooks County received scholarships from the foundation, mostly to attend Texas A&M University in Kingsville. In addition, the foundation helped fund a Nautical Archeology Series at A&M University in College Station as well as a children's home in Beeville.

Mr. Ed was born into an educated ranching family in Rockport, Texas, in 1878. He graduated from Bayview College in Portland, Texas, and worked on ranches in Texas and Oklahoma. He once went on a trail ride in his younger years, and he eventually came to Falfurrias in 1904. He married Louise Allen, a schoolteacher, in 1912. His brand was Y, a continuation of his father's brand. He was a mason. He died in a car accident in 1964.

He was truly memorable not only to people in our hometown but also to many others who benefited from his generosity.

# A THIRD GRADER'S EYE VIEW

When I was in the third grade in Falfurrias, I was allowed to walk the two blocks from school to my father's office by myself in the afternoons. My father had a real estate and cattle loan business in an office behind the Falfurrias First National Bank building. I waited at the office until he was ready to leave work and drive me and my brother and sister home. From school, I walked across the courthouse grounds, which at that time extended much farther east than now. The numerous sidewalks on the grounds made it possible to take different paths and find interesting, new walks. Many of the plants on the grounds were oleanders. The courthouse stood on a high place and was the tallest building in town. It looked so beautiful and grand.

There was little traffic, but I was cautious when I crossed the streets—those were my instructions. There were two streets to cross before coming to Rice Street, the "Main Street." The bank (on a corner on the north side of Rice Street) was a big and impressive building with its tall columns. Sometimes I stopped to touch the smooth round columns; they were so cold in winter and could be very hot in warm weather. I always entered the office quietly because there was often a conversation going on between my father and a client or someone who was just visiting. My father had a reputation for having good judgment, and folks often came by to ask his advice on their business matters, especially farming and cattle raising.

When the weather was rainy or cold, I stayed in the office and usually sat close to the window so I could see the people walking by outside. Sometimes I just watched the secretary, Mary Maupin, type. She typed so fast! Her fingers flew, and she never seemed to stop to erase anything. Sometimes she stopped to talk and ask me about school and my dogs. When the weather was warm and nice, I ventured a short way to the north of the office and visited with Mr. Cone, the shoe repairman. He had white hair, wore a big leather apron, and was always smiling. His door was kept open; either he wanted to catch the cool breeze from the east. or he wanted folks to feel welcome. His little shop had that great smell of leather. He liked to talk to visitors, but he never stopped working.

If my sister was with me, we sometimes walked from the office the one block east on Rice Street. I always wanted to look behind the Mercantile Hardware where the old Falfurrias Mercantile Store had been before it burned. There was a large, deep, hollow space that had been the store basement. It held a special fascination.

We could see the train depot across the railroad tracks. Sometimes a freight train would rumble in. The passenger trains came through at night. The engines were so big and loud that I feared them. I was convinced that their smoke went into the sky to make rain clouds.

We then crossed the street and went to the post office to check box 266. When we looked through the window to the inside, we often saw Mr. Sloan, the postmaster. He had lots of white hair and a big smile when he looked up and saw us.

After, we crossed back to the north side of Rice Street. As we walked west along Rice Street, we passed the Falfurrias Hardware where our friend Albert Dale worked. If we saw him at all, he was busy and involved or walking with his quick step to the next customer. Farther to the west was the Falfurrias Creamery that seemed to scent the air with the smell of fresh butter—or did we imagine that? Often, Nat Best, Sr., one of two black men in town, was standing out on the sidewalk of the creamery. Nat was a pleasant and jolly fellow. He worked at the creamery and was a driver for Mr. Lasater. He seemed to know everyone, and they knew him and usually stopped to talk to him. Then there was the telegraph office where messages were still being sent in Morse code and then translated. The operator stuttered, and it was said that his dot-dashes stuttered, too. The Jungeman Bakery was in the same block. It filled the air with the fresh aroma of bread and pastries. Our family ate their hamburger buns toasted for breakfast; we thought they were much too tasty to use only for hamburgers.

The Perez drugstore was on the west corner of the same block and had a soda fountain with a reputation for the best limeades in town. It sold a few gifts and indulgences like men's Old Spice cologne and Ladies' Evening in Paris perfume. As far as I knew, those were the only perfumes and fragrances in town. The Poole jewelry store was across the street to the south, as was Califa's Apparel. Most Falfurrias men wore tan Stetsons or Dobbs hats, which they usually bought at Califa's. When the men would return favors amongst themselves, they often did it with the gift of a hat. "Go find you a hat at Califa's" was the word.

Mr. Hise's barbershop was near Califa's. When children went into the shop for their haircuts, they were put onto the little board that lifted them in the barber chair. Every little girl I knew went to Mr. Hise and had a short bob and bangs. Mr. Hise collected tarantulas, and he kept them in jars in his shop. We saw him on Sundays, too, because he had a great voice and sang in and directed the church choir. Every Christmas he was Santa at the Baptist Church Christmas program. His disguise didn't really work; the children all knew who he was. Behind Mr. Hise's shop was the Gee Cleaners. A cloud of steam seemed to rise continually from the cleaners, and a distinctive blend of hot steam and hair lotion smells drifted onto the street.

Piggly Wiggly grocery store was on the south side of Rice Street, and was operated by Mr. Hassel, Mr. Tease, and Mr. Sorenson. It served us well if we ate mostly canned food. Fresh produce never seemed quite fresh unless it came from our gardens.

Hobbs, on the north side of Rice Street, was our dry goods store. It sold ladies', men's, children's, and babies' clothing and accessories. It had shelves filled with bolts of material, and it had tables where ladies sat to look at dress pattern books. Women sewed many of their own clothes, so they pondered over the right material and color for the season and then searched for the just-right pattern to use. The manager was named Mauricio, and he seemed to be able to answer all questions, and even make suggestions when we came in to shop for a gift.

To the west there was the picture show. Every Saturday there was a matinee with a Western movie. My grandmother loved Westerns, so she took my brother, sister, and me with her each Saturday. There was always a serial show as well as the feature film— the kind that ended each episode with impending doom. In the movies, the same plots seemed to play each Saturday, but we would have been disappointed with anything else. After the movie, Grandmother would take us to a little candy store just off Rice Street. She bought us rock candy (little clustered chunks of crystallized sugar.) It was her favorite. Licorice was absolutely forbidden.

Sometimes we crossed from the picture show to the south side of Rice Street, turned left, and passed the Falfurrias Facts office where Mr. Dickey was editor of the paper. As we walked toward Belton's drugstore, we passed Dr. Otken's office. It was a small frame building that people rarely visited because Dr. Otken made house calls. For me, visits to his office usually called for little powders wrapped in paper and a throat swabbing.

Next to Dr. Otken's office was Belton's drugstore. When we walked inside, we saw stuffed wild animals staring down at us, along with mounted animal heads with huge antlers and enormous stuffed rattlesnakes on display. The sight of all the creatures was shocking and fearsome and contrasted with the delightful fragrance of vanilla that seemed to permeate the store. We usually got cones at the soda fountain. I always ordered a pineapple sherbet "ice cream" cone and realized years later why the soda fountain fellow seemed amused. The cones were five cents.

After the stop at Belton's we again crossed Rice Street and went to our father's office. Downtown Falfurrias was two blocks long, but it was the center of our world.

*"Riding in Style"*

# GOING PLACES

In the 1920s and 1930s, when people went somewhere, it was usually in an open car. Even with a top cover on the automobile, we felt the sun, the cold, and the rain. In summer, we girls dressed in sundresses and welcomed the wind with little consideration for our hair getting blown around. On cold winter days, we wore coats, caps, and sometimes gloves. And for times of heavy rain, cars were equipped with see-through window covers that snapped on. The transparent parts of the covers were made of icing glass (made from the mineral mica). When not being used, the covers were kept under the seats of the car. Also under the front seat was the crank. Inserting the crank in the slot in front of the motor and then giving it a fast circle with the arm would get the motor started. The car also had a jack for changing a flat tire, patches and paste to put on any holes in the inner tube and coveralls to give protection for the dirty job. On any long trip, at least one flat tire could be expected. The spare tire was attached upright at the back of the car.

We had never heard of seatbelts or car seats for children. The adults held the small children, and when they got a little older, they sat on the seats or on a larger person's lap. Lots of people could ride in one vehicle. Young children took turns standing up in back—that's where they could see the most.

The running board on each side of the car served an important purpose; people stepped up on it to get in the seat. It was dangerous for them, but little dogs often liked to ride on the running boards. It was a good place to carry a block of ice from the icehouse to home. If a car was moving slowly, a young man might jump onto the running board and ride along—especially if he liked the young lady driver.

At one point, my family inherited a second car. It was a little two-door Ford. In the back was a rumble seat where the trunk would be in cars today.

It was a pull-up seat that opened for a ride in the open air. Two people could sit in the seat if they were small. Some acrobatics were required to get into it, but it was a fun ride. Everyone referred to the little car as a "friendly" car because people always waved to folks in the rumble seat.

In South Texas, we had quite narrow highways. Highways 281 and 285 crossed at Falfurrias. The highways and two or three major streets in town were paved, but mostly the streets were gravel or dirt, and country roads were stretches of sand with convenient ruts for one car. If two cars met, one driver would politely pull outside the sandy path—and hope not to get stuck. If a car was stuck in the sand or mud, a person would use a shovel or put boards in front of the front wheels to give a smooth run out.

For our family, a trip to visit my father's brother Robert in the Rio Grande Valley was like traveling in a maze of sunflowers. The highway (281) south of Falfurrias was unpaved until the late 1920s. The sunflowers towered above the car and were so thick we saw little else along the way. To see an occasional windmill was reassuring; that meant we could probably get water for the car if it heated up.

Sometimes we took trips to Kingsville, Texas, to visit a dentist or to shop. As we came into Kingsville from the west, I heard my parents refer to the King Ranch. That was how I knew a king had a ranch in South Texas. In fact, I could see the tower of his castle. (Actually it was the main house of the King Ranch.) In Kingsville, we always stopped at Ragland's store where the gracious ladies and the man selling shoes were especially friendly. The store had a pleasant distinctive fragrance and a fascinating gadget—a kind of capsule that carried checks and money to a cashier on the second floor. It traveled on a cable and sailed into the air and then came back on a cable. Across the street, the post office lawn had lots of beautiful palm trees and an interesting fence with heavy chains going from one post to another. But best of all was the little pool with gold fish that was on the grounds. Then we always went to eat at the White Kitchen restaurant where the floor was checkered with little black and white tiles.

We had to get an early start when going to Corpus Christi, whether to visit Dr. Heaney or Lichtenstein's department store. My family thought Lichtenstein's was the finest store in all of South Texas. They knew the clerks and the elevator man by name. Richardson's was the place to buy shoes, and the Nueces Hotel was the best place to eat lunch. At the Nueces Hotel, the dining room was a bright partial circle that was mostly windows. After a meal, the waiter would bring "finger bowls" with warm water to each person. Sometimes we ate at a restaurant right on the waterfront. There we could marvel at and admire the huge mounted fish. It would be nighttime when we finally got home.

A trip to San Antonio started very early, too. And a trip to Houston sometimes took two days. On the way, we children enjoyed counting the cows and horses in the fields—and if we spotted a white horse, we could make a wish. We liked reading the billboards. Camel and Lucky Strike cigarettes both had big billboard signs, as did Coca-Cola. We also liked looking at little signs like Eat at Mom's Café, but our favorites were the Burma Shave signs, a series of little signs that rhymed. For example: Grandpa's beard ... Was stiff and coarse ... And that's what ... Caused ... His fifth divorce ... *Burma Shave*. Or another one: No lady likes ... To dance ... Or dine ... Accompanied by ... A porcupine ... *Burma Shave*.

If we went to San Antonio or Houston, we stayed with relatives for a few days and enjoyed the wonders of the cities. Our San Antonio aunt made sure we took the pilgrimage to the Alamo, and we often went to the Brackenridge Zoo. We never grew tired of seeing the animals and roaming the park. In the evenings, it was a thrill to drive up Broadway and see the lights. In Falfurrias we had our starry nights, but we loved the dazzling colorful lights of the city.

When we were visiting Houston, we often went to Galveston to swim. The waves were a new and exciting sensation, as we had known only the earthen tanks in Falfurrias. I asked my mother if the water in Galveston was over my head in the middle, and she assured me that it was. In Houston, too, we children loved the bright lights and always requested a drive down Main Street in the evening.

My Falfurrias High School English teacher, Miss Martin Holbrook, had spent time in New York City and talked about its wondrous attractions. We students knew New York City was a famous place, and she made it sound truly exciting and sparked our interest to travel to faraway places. But it was not until after graduation from high school in 1940 that my sister Catherine and I had a chance to go outside of Texas. We went to Taos, New Mexico, to visit an aunt and her family. The tall mountains—and mountains behind mountains—amazed us. The streams, rivers, and trees were incredibly beautiful. The roads, however, were hazardous; they were narrow with sharp curves and often built on a mountain shelf with a deep drop on one side. It made folks from flat land South Texas close their eyes and say a prayer.

During World War II, my navy officer husband and I lived in New York City for a short while and found it spectacular with its tremendous size, convenient subways, fabulous museums, elegant theatres, famous performers, and delicious food. We later visited and explored a lot more of the world, but we eventually came back to South Texas to stay. Today, there are still some sandy roads, but a person has to search to find them.

*Uncle Joe Myrick and "Ranchero"*

# SUMMER EVENING CONVERSATIONS

After supper on summer evenings in deep South Texas, my family, sometimes with friends and neighbors, found the cooling breezes on our lawns or porches and sat together and relaxed. In the twilight we often marveled at the pink sweeps of afterglow from the fiery flame of a brilliant sunset. The conversations of the older folks would meander through their memories and brush country wisdoms. It was the 1920s and 1930s, and it seemed we were all comfortable in our little part of the world.

We children spent time chasing the lightning bugs and playing with the dogs, and then we would stop and rest and listen to the stories and musings of the older generations. My grandfather, Henry Thomas, sometimes recalled living in the Washington Territory and felling the giant trees for his home and for sale to the sawmills. and he would tell how only oxen were used to pull wagons and sleds because they were surefooted and did not stumble over the tree stumps. My aunt, Drusilla Myrick, his daughter, also remembered living in the Territory and walking miles on trails in the woods with her older sister to visit their aunt. She talked about how they felt terror whenever they came across an Indian man and walked fast with eyes downcast until they got beyond him—and then they ran as fast as they could. There were stories about white children who had been kidnapped. But it was an Indian woman who attended my grandmother at the birth of several of her children. And it was the Indian women who taught the settler women how to dry fruit on the roofs of their houses and how to make hominy from corn.

Other Washington Territory stories told of ventures into the forests where panthers were seen watering at the streams. At such times, the children knew to be absolutely still, to make no movement until the animal had gone. And there were bears.

The bears liked to climb the same fruit and berry trees as the children. My aunt once looked up and saw a little black bear above her in the tree she was climbing to gather berries. Sightings of large bears brought real panic. It was two forest fires and a debilitating case of measles that brought my grandfather and his family back to Texas after nine years in the North Country. On the way from the Washington Territory, their train was snowbound for days in Colorado. The male passengers—young and old—helped dig, and they finally cleared the tracks.

My grandfather told stories of going on a cattle drive from Ft. Worth to Abilene, Kansas, when he was a very young man. He said that when the nights were cold he made a cow that was lying down get up and move so he could then bed down on the warm spot where the cow had been. He remembered sliding off the back of his horse and holding onto its tail when they had to cross swollen rivers.

Grandmother Thomas loved to tell the story about the horses from their ranch at Veal Station, Texas, being stolen at night—by Indians. Her father decided to sleep on the porch one night with the end of a rope tied to his leg and the other end of the rope tied to a horse in the horse pen; that way he would know if anyone disturbed the horses. The next morning, the rope was cut and the horse was gone—and he had slept on.

Uncle Joe Myrick who was married to my Aunt Drusilla ("Auntie") had some fascinating stories. As a very young boy, he sailed with his family from Liverpool, England, and remembered wearing a Little-Lord-Fauntleroy-type velvet suit on the way and being tied to the ship so he would not fall in the sea. He came to Falfurrias as a young man in his twenties, by way of Canada and San Antonio. He remembered how an Indian woman in Winnipeg, Manitoba, rubbed his face with snow to warm him when he was shivering with the cold.

Before he ran the Park Hotel in Falfurrias and then became a dairyman and farmer, Uncle Joe worked as a ranch hand in South Texas and also herded mules from one location to another for ranchers. He carried a bedroll and slept wherever he was when nightfall came. One night back when Oakville, Texas, was a county seat, he stopped there to spend the night on the courthouse grounds. A prisoner called from a jail window and asked for a cigarette. Uncle Joe gave him one and lit it. Early the next morning, Uncle Joe woke up to many voices and much commotion—the courtyard was full of people. When Joe asked why so many people were there, he was told, "There's going to be a hanging." Joe had given a last cigarette to the fellow that was hung.

Uncle Joe remembered driving his horse and buggy to meet every train when he ran the Park Hotel. Many of the passengers who got off the train were coming to see Don Pedrito, a local *curandero*. Don Pedrito's reputation as a healer was widely known. Joe told of a man he knew who had a bad skin condition on his feet that wouldn't heal. He was cured after he followed Don Pedrito's advice to empty a can of tomatoes in each of his boots, put the boots on his feet, and leave them on for a week.

After the Galveston storm in 1900, Joe went to Galveston to help bury the dead and assist with the clearing. He said he could never forget the horror he found. In South Texas he became a skilled horseman and hunter and a baseball pitcher for weekend games—he also loved to tell how fast he could run. Upon request, Joe would sing some of the old cowboy songs and recite poems he had learned years before. He could still recite "Face on the Barroom Floor" when he was close to ninety years old.

My mother, Annie Mae, and Joe enjoyed reminiscing about their early years in San Antonio. They had not known each other at the time, but they were both there when the center of the town was near the Alamo, Commerce Street, and the Menger Hotel. On Saturdays, Mother and her brother and sister walked from their home on Cypress Street (north of the town center on Tobin Hill) to their father's music store on Commerce Street.

She remembered going to parties in the Menger Hotel, and Joe remembered how he had shined shoes near the Alamo. He was at the Menger Hotel when Teddy Roosevelt was there recruiting for the Rough Riders who would later go to fight for Cuba during the Spanish American War. He talked about the time Don Pedrito was in San Antonio and people camped near the Alamo for days to be near him.

Mother remembered stories her father had told of his early days in San Antonio. He was amazed at the large number of donkeys used to carry and deliver wood and water. Her father was impressed with the rigged harnesses on the animals—so makeshift and original. Her father had come to San Antonio from Mississippi in 1882. He found Texas bustling, exciting and full of promise.

World War I was still fresh in their memories. Everyone seemed to think the United States would always be safe from attack and that the war had truly made the whole world safe. Jim Lackey, an older cousin, was often among us. He had been in the navy during World War I and spent some time in Europe. He spoke with great confidence that the French Maginot Line (a line of defenses) was absolute protection for France. My grandfather was a rather quiet man, but he had studied Bible prophesy, and during such conversations he often said, "Watch out for Russia."

Salt Lake, south of Falfurrias, was a great source of legends that people believed with conviction. One part of the lake was said to be bottomless.

Local residents had dived deep and never reached the bottom. And then there was a story about someone seeing horse-drawn buggy tracks leading into the lake and never turning around or appearing on the other side.

Throughout the evenings, the adults exchanged brush country wisdoms, and agreement was usually unanimous. Putting up fences had caused the creeks in South Texas to run dry! Someone had sighted a cross between a humming bird and a butterfly. Horsetail hairs turned into little snakes when they got in the water troughs. The rattles of a male rattlesnake were turned vertically and those of a female were horizontal. Mules were much smarter than horses. On a moonlit night, someone might comment that "Scientists say people will fly to the moon someday." Then there might be a soft chuckling because everyone knew that could never happen. One of the wisdoms from Uncle Joe was in Spanish—*"Borregos en el cielo, agua en el suelo,"* meaning "sheep (small puffy clouds close together) in the sky, water (rain) in the ground." This seemed to be true; a few days after such cloud formations, it would rain.

My father, John, liked to remember that when the family lived in North Texas he rode a horse when doing errands. He was so young that he couldn't possibly reach the stirrups of the saddle. He just held onto the saddle horn. Fortunately, the horse always seemed to know where he should go. And my father was proud that as a young teenager he was the fastest in the family at shearing sheep. He also loved telling us about a train trip he took when he worked at the bank in Falfurrias. He had gone with a group of dairy farmers to the Rocky Mountains. He saw Yellowstone Park, swam in the Great Salt Lake, and experienced the grandeur of the Rocky Mountains. It was fascinating to hear tales of travels.

Auntie, Drusilla Myrick, would have been the first to say she was not superstitious, but along the way she had lots of advice and cautions. She let us know we should never start a new project on Friday. She warned us that a pregnant woman should never look at a deformed or retarded person for fear of passing something abnormal to her unborn child. And she was adamant about a person not sleeping where moonlight could shine on them; it could make them strange. She had been a nurse and had endless remedies to recommend for animals as well as people. She successfully took care of snakebites with "coal oil." She had a purple ointment that she used on chickens, horses, cows, and dogs that seemed to heal and protect their wounds. Each spring, on Auntie's advice, we children were given sulfur tablets to chew. I do not know why. There was also "chill tonic," a liquid with little crystal-like granules. Castor oil was not overlooked. Sometimes she insisted we had to take it, too. Also, she was a beekeeper and thought honey was absolutely the purest of foods and could cure almost any ailment.

All of the older folks were pioneers. One was a pioneer who came to the New World, others to a homestead in uncharted territory, and all of them were pioneers in South Texas. They seemed happy and optimistic, confident they had found a good new life. We children felt that we were a part of it. Our older generations gave us so much that seemed to define the family and trigger our imaginations. And we learned that there was a world beyond our brush country that we, too, might explore someday.

# WINDOWS OPEN TO THE WORLD

There was a time in South Texas when people kept the windows and doors of their homes and businesses open most of the year. Screens kept the insects out, and the breeze was welcome—it was our way to stay cool. It also let the outside in, making us more a part of the world outside.

Everyone in towns and for miles into the countryside could hear the twelve-noon whistle blow. It divided our day and signaled that it was time to go home and have lunch. Schools did not serve meals, so on school days, the children dashed home or their parents picked them up and drove them home. Many of the fathers with businesses in town closed up and went home for lunch, too.

With our windows open, we could easily hear the fire alarm siren. If we were home, there would be a rush out of the house to look for the smoke, followed by speculation as to whose house or business was burning. One of the most exciting sounds was that of an airplane, which would bring the whole family outside. The planes were usually bi-planes with two wings, so when we saw one with only one wing, we talked about the "new" kind of airplane we saw. Occasionally, a plane would land at our Falfurrias landing strip and take people for a ride. It would cost about a dollar and half.

Another sound imprinted in my memory is the delicate high-pitch tinkling that was heard when the soft breezes stirred the glass wind chimes in our dining room archway. And then in the heat of the afternoon, I could hear the slow, soft, sleepy call of the Inca doves. Some of the night noises are the most memorable. On our little farm, you could hear the sound of the steady rhythm of the windmill as its pump caused a clinking of one pipe bobbing into another. And from the big earthen water tank, you could hear the low drone of the frogs as they sent out their croaking calls to one another. Early in the night, you could hear the whip-poor-wills and the great horned owls that nested in the tall eucalyptus tree.

When there was moonlight, we could sometimes hear a mocking bird serenading the night. When the temperature was very warm, cicadas sang in a loud chorus. We wondered how they all knew to start and stop at the same time. And the coyotes, which ran in packs and howled at times, yapped and barked all together as they chased through the fields. Toward sun-up, mother cows let out urgent calls, and their calves seemed to answer. Then we usually heard a rooster announce the morning, sometimes among our chickens and sometimes in the distance.

It was reassuring to hear the train whistles. We knew the one very late at night was the passenger train heading north, and the one just before daylight was the one heading south.

During watermelon season and other fruit and vegetable gathering times, extra workers were brought in, and on Saturday nights they gathered in open pastures to eat and drink together—and maybe to wager on dice or card games. Toward midnight, trucks took the workers to their lodgings, and on their way, they sang. Their voices drifted in the quiet night, and we could hear their beautiful songs and happy *gritos* as the trucks passed by on the road beyond our house.

In springtime, our open windows let us smell the delightful fragrance of the orange blossoms. It was like a lovely caress. And with the southeast breeze sometimes came the smell of freshly plowed earth and mowed grass, with just a hint of the salt water from the bay beyond. We began our summer nights in bed with no covers, comfortable with the feel of the breeze over us. We felt a part of the seasons and the world outside that was alive and awake.

*"Fluffy"*

# FLUFFY

---

Fluffy was my first dog. She was given to our family when she was a tiny bouncing ball of white fur—a gift from a Falfurrias family named Fenstra. They told us she was a combination of Chihuahua and Spitz. She stayed small and became my shadow as the two of us roamed, explored, and discovered the corners and fields on our little farm. She developed a strong and protective territorial sense and seemed to know instinctively that possums that came sneaking in the night should not be in her territory. She barked in a great frenzied fury when they were eating the oranges on the trees, continuing until my father came outside. Then she ran to the tree with the possum. Sometimes my father grabbed the creature by the tail and bashed its head. Other times he got his gun while Fluffy kept the animal frightened and in the tree until it was disposed of. Then she would grab it by its neck and shake it in her mouth, growling as if to say, "So there!" Afterwards, she walked away, wagging her tail slowly and panting a little.

She was always loving with our family and polite to our friends, but when strangers came, she greeted them with fierce barking.

One evening in the late 1920s, our family came home from visiting friends, and Fluffy met us with urgent barking and bouncing. At first we thought she was just so glad to see us, but then we realized she was more excited than usual. Was she trying to tell us something? We went into our house, and Fluffy kept barking. My father went outside to see if there was a possum in an orange tree, and Fluffy ran toward the house of the farm helper, Julian Palacios and his wife Cristila. My father followed her as far as the gate to their yard, but he did not want to disturb them, so he came back to our house. Fluffy would not be quiet; she kept barking. Again, my father went outside, and again she ran toward Julian's house. My father came back and went to bed.

Early the next morning, Julian came to tell us that someone had come into his house the night before, blew out the lamp, and went toward the bed. Cristela saw the man and screamed. Then he dashed out of the house. After hearing the story, my father called the sheriff, Jesse Grimes, and he and a deputy came out to the farm. With Fluffy by their side, they found foot tracks, traced the tracks, and found the thief trying to hide in our back pasture brush. He surrendered easily when he saw big Jesse Grimes with his pistol drawn. They brought the fellow back toward our house in handcuffs, his hair hanging down and his head bent. Fluffy wagged her tail as if to say, "Here he is!" Among other confessions, the robber said he tried to break into our house, but "the little dog would not let me."

Jesse Grimes reminded us that houses in town had been broken into and people had had money stolen. Folks there were sitting on their porches or lawns with their guns ready to protect their homes. The fellow in handcuffs was the thief. He had come into the country after people in town took up arms.

My aunt had a white Spitz male dog and at times she kept Fluffy to breed with her Spitz. They had beautiful little puppies almost every spring. For me, and for my friends, it was more fun to play with them than with dolls. We dressed them in doll clothes and carried them around in doll buggies and wagons. They were our real live babies, and with them we played out our make-believe scenarios.

Our family always found good homes for the puppies, but there was one that I could not part with—Buster. He was especially dear, so he became my second little shadow. He was quick to learn tricks—rolling over, shaking hands, walking on hind legs, and sitting up. He could also climb. He climbed up haystacks and some of the shorter trees with me. He, too, became a threat to the possums—but he didn't just bark. He grabbed them by the neck, shook them, and would not let go!

Every morning before breakfast, I went outside to greet Buster and give him a hug. One morning when I called, he did not come. My father came out of the house with tears in his eyes, put his arms around me, and told me Buster had been shot. He was already buried. My small world crashed. He was so precious—so innocent—and I loved him so. Through my tears, I saw Fluffy slowly come up to me, and she seemed as sad as I was. We consoled each other. Buster had been fighting with a possum the night before and then was hit by a shotgun blast my grandfather had intended for the possum. It was a sad day for the whole family, but especially for my grandfather.

When Fluffy was about five years old, she was hit by a car. She lived on with only three good legs. The accident barely slowed her down after she healed. She could still run, continue her possum patrols, and have beautiful puppies. She lived to be an old dog age—lively and alert all of her years.

*Out By the Tank*

# OUT BY THE TANK

In the Falfurrias early days, even though a farm might be small, if there were cattle, horses, or mules, there was also an earthen tank where the animals watered and cooled off in the summer heat. In other areas, a tank might be called a pond, and some of ours were large enough to be called ponds. They were dug-out areas with mounds of dirt forming the banks. To make sure there was always enough water in the tank, the windmill ran almost constantly, pumping water into it much of the time. Our tank nurtured a complete cycle of life for aquatic and amphibious creatures.

The tanks were alluring attractions for children. On our farm, the tank had been in its location long enough to have large colonies of water creatures. Tall hackberry trees stood on the banks with long branches that draped almost into the water. When approaching the tank, we children usually walked up the bank slowly and quietly, hoping we would not frighten the creatures. Sometimes the bank near the water's edge was lined with turtles, and as soon as our heads came into their view, they scuttled and disappeared quickly into the water. But it would not be long before their heads popped up to peer above the surface. Occasionally, we had the thrill of seeing a baby turtle, and then we would try to catch it so we could take it to our house, admire it and pamper it by feeding it flies.

Frogs, too, sunned on the banks, and when people approached, hundreds of frogs leapt in unison and splashed into the water. Afterwards, some of them stuck their head out of the water. We liked to look carefully at the heads because we sometimes imagined we saw a snake. We could not be sure unless it swam in a snake-like wiggle. At the edge of the water and especially in the shade of the trees, there were swarms of minnows. They, too, left quickly when people appeared. Bigger fish flipped and splashed in the water, and in our childhood wisdom, we knew they were the parents of the minnows.

The smooth water was a perfect reflector of the trees and sky, disturbed only by the little rings moving away from the spots where dragonflies dipped their tails into the water. Birds loved the place. They perched on the low branches and fluttered into a spin to snap up the flying insects. Other large long-legged gray and white birds waded in the shallows or just stood motionless. Sometimes we saw rare birds like the gallinule; they never seemed to be disturbed even when people came near. They just kept wading and looking down, searching the water.

At night, noises came from the tank. The sound of a deep voice croaking was thought to be the big daddy or grandfather frog. And then there were the high-pitched sounds of many frogs together. We thought these were the young frogs joining in a chorus. Along with the sounds of the water creatures, we could hear the steady, slow clinking of the windmill, always pumping and always nurturing with fresh water.

*Birdie Bell Riley*

# FALFURRIAS FIRST BAPTIST CHURCH

The Falfurrias First Baptist Church held its 100th Anniversary Celebration on July 23rd, 2006. The anniversary was a time to remember all the past ministers, the songs sung throughout the years, and the people who contributed to the mission of the church with their vision, encouragement, and the examples of their lives.

With the education building filled to capacity and overflowing to standing-room-only, the anniversary observance began at 10 AM and lasted until after 4 PM. We sang many of the old songs. The glorious voices of Esther, Dorothy, and Janie Minten led us in "Precious Memories" and songs from seven different hymnals that we had used through the years.

Martha Hise Flaming, who was the talented and faithful church pianist for decades, played old favorites on the piano. Former and present members of the choir gathered to sing one of the hymns together. Some of us thought of Willie Fitzhenry and Kathlyn Ward who had added their voices to the choir. In my mind, I could hear my father singing as we sang. The fact that he could not carry a tune never stopped him; he loved to sing out! I remembered how he had taught a boy's Sunday school class for years, was a deacon, and served as church treasurer for thirty-one years.

Among the memories shared were those of the children's songs we sang in Sunday school and the Bible stories that came alive back then. And we remembered that during the church services, elderly men were often called on topray—especially Mr. Keener, Mr. Burdett, and my grandfather, Henry Thomas. They knelt and prayed on and on with such deep reverence and sincerity.

We recalled how everyone was so very pleased and proud of our church when it was newly built. Its beautiful and delicate colors, edged in gold, decorated the inside and matched the colors in the glass windows. A lovely painting of a flowing stream hung at the back of the baptistery. Before the new church was built, people were baptized in the Scaggs' tank west of town. We remembered some of the revival preachers, Brother Baucum in particular. After evening services, he used to join the hound dog hunters on their wolf hunts—and eventually got the hunters to come to church services.

Ann Zahn was recognized as being the oldest person attending at ninety-two years of age. A six-month-old baby was the youngest. Martha Hise Flaming had two of her out-of-town brothers with her, Lynn and Ross. Some of the others from early days that returned for the anniversary were Elizabeth Dale Tarr, Olivia Williams Schnitz, Margie P. Calahan, Katy Otken Branch, Bob Hicks, Fay Elizabeth Harder Smith, Dorothy Harder Smith, Lois Maun Jackson, and Jon Ryan.

We recalled past members, including Mr. Hise who led the choir, Mrs. Falkenburg who played the piano, and Mrs. McCullar and Mrs. Burdett who carried their Bibles and "quarterlies" because they taught Sunday school. On the left side of the church and toward the front, Mrs. Hise used to sit with her row of little boys, and a few pews behind her, Mrs. Ryan sat with her little redheaded boys. Then a little farther back Mrs. Otken sat with her sons and Katy, and Mrs. Maun sat with her daughters. The Glassner Family, Leota Dale, Lella Bell Wright, and Mrs. Riley also sat on the left side of the church. My parents sat on the right side. When children got older—perhaps in their teens—they sat together toward the back of the church.

Most of the year, our church windows stayed open during services. Since we did not have air-conditioning, we used little hand fans that were kept in the songbook racks. Local businesses usually supplied them and advertised on the back of the fan.

One of the early members of the church was Birdie Bell Riley. She was truly a presence and in my memory a very prim and sedate lady always dressed in what was thought to be the latest fashion. She wore beautiful hats to church, decorated with bows and flowers and veils. She taught a young ladies' Sunday school class (the Alathean class) for years. As the young ladies grew older, they stayed on in the class because they did not want to leave Mrs. Riley. My parents knew Birdie Bell and her husband Will when they first came to Falfurrias and remembered them as a fun-loving, young married couple. They did not have children, and Will died early in their marriage. Birdie Bell stayed on in their Falfurrias home and spent the rest of her life devoted to her church, active in the community, busy covering buttons and making buttonholes for people—back in the days when women sewed many of their own clothes. A collection of old pictures show Birdie Bell on a horse and carrying a shotgun, and even then she was well dressed!

It was a joy to be among people from the past, in a place that was such a part of our growth, and to remember the folks who inspired us.

# MY FIRST BEST FRIEND

Marie Bennett and I could never remember when we first became friends. As far back as memory took us, we had shared our time, our secrets, and our flights of imagination. In our earliest years together, we played with baby dolls and puppies in our wagons and doll carriages. We made houses with cardboard boxes, wooden orange crates, and firewood logs. Whatever we did on the farm, we shared with my dog Fluffy; Fluffy insisted on being included.

Later, paper dolls came into our lives. We had paper dolls of the Dion Quintuplets first. We knew their names and could tell them apart. We made paper dollhouses out of shoeboxes and smaller boxes, and then later had small dollhouses and little furniture. Our paper dolls seemed to grow up as we grew. Finally they were grown, dating, and getting married. Once, in the soft magical glow of Christmas lights, we played out our pretend lives under the Christmas tree after I had gotten some tiny furniture as a present.

We also set up little farms and ranches in shady places outside. An empty log cabin syrup container made the perfect house. Trees could be any twigs of greenery. Fences were matchsticks with string looped around them. And the animals were empty thread spools with twisted pipe cleaners to make their legs and heads. Spools were different sizes for different animals. An oval empty sardine can pushed into the sand made a perfect tank.

On occasion, we spent time thinking and talking about the why questions. We knew God made everything happen, but we wondered why he put us inside our skin and not somebody else's. Why were we put into our families? And why were we put into our town? How did God decide?

Since God could do anything, it was not startling when Mother told me where babies came from. She told me God planted a seed next to the mother's heart, and when the seed had grown into a baby, God provided a way for the baby to come into the world. Eventually, an older girlfriend gave me an explanation with more details. I firmly denied her story. I told her, "Not in my family." After that I went to Mother with new questions, and she expanded upon her original story. I then realized my parents had made a baby four times because there were four of us children.

Marie and I took piano lessons from Marie's mother, Mary Bell. We loved the idea of being able to play well, but I spent more time with my horse than the piano. After giving up the piano, Marie took violin lessons and later clarinet. She went on to play in a band, and I became a twirler. Years later after I was married and living in the North Country, my Mother wrote to me saying, "Someone wants to buy your piano. And another person wants to buy your horse. Should we sell them?" I wrote back, "Sell the piano. Keep the horse."

Marie and I were excited when we heard Buster Brown was going to visit Falfurrias. He came and performed on the stage of our movie theater. He was the midget mascot of Buster Brown shoes. He wore a red suit with Knickerbocker pants, a tam on his blond bobbed hair, and black patent leather shoes. He danced in his Buster Brown shoes and told jokes. After the performance, Marie and I found him leaving out the back of the theater. I was so anxious to talk to him. After we caught up with him, I got his attention and told him, "I have a dog named Buster." I thought he would be pleased and recognize it as a compliment. He didn't even smile. When we were up close, I realized he was a wrinkled little old man—not the cute little boy in the pictures.

Marie and I often worked as a team in school. We made posters and wrote stories and plays together. We were paired in plays and presentations. We both remember the little dance performance where the girls had boy partners. I got to dance with Joe Downs. Years later, Marie told me she had wanted to dance with Joe!

I was with Marie when I fell off a seesaw and broke my arm. We walked to her house nearby, her mother took me to the doctor, and I was in a temporary cast and sling before my family knew what had happened. Joe was the sweet young fellow who carried my books until I had two good arms again.

When we got to the seventh grade, we were in the high school building and got to go to chapel once a week. I have long forgotten most of the programs, speeches, and speakers, but I still hear the songs we sang—"The Spanish Cavalier," "Sailing," "Santa Lucia," "Drink to me Only with Thine

Eyes," rounds, Christmas songs, and all the patriotic songs. One time in chapel, we were shown a new device called a television. We saw a speckled picture on a big screen, and they said that having such pictures (there was no sound) in our homes was in our future.

In high school, Marie and I were Home Economics partners. Since neither of us had domestic inclinations at that time, it was all new to us. Though we read recipes and did our best to follow them, we were dismal failures at cooking. However, we did get one "A" on a breakfast presentation; it was shredded wheat and bananas. Our teacher said we arranged it in the bowl very artistically. Our sewing projects were never showpieces, but we did get compliments on our nice, small stitches in the hems (done by hand.) We both worked on our high school paper and found we were better at writing than the Home Economics projects.

Marie and I reached a time when it was so hard to be serious on solemn occasions. During our seventh-grade graduation, our class was on the high school stage with the speaker, the superintendent, and the principal. As we watched the speaker rock back and forth on his feet as he spoke, the situation became so funny! Marie and I looked at each other. That was a mistake—we burst out laughing. Thankfully the speaker was about finished, and soon the clapping from the audience drowned out our laughter.

We were the two junior bridesmaids in our music teacher's wedding, "Miss Gladys" Sparks, who married John Morgan Brooks. Marie and I finally stifled our laughs at the altar after giggling our way down the aisle.

Marie and I were often mistaken for each other. Our size and coloring were much the same. Our fathers were somewhat similar in stature, which added to the confusion. I was sometimes asked if my father was the postmaster in Falfurrias (Mr. Bennett was); Marie was asked if her father was in real estate (my father was).

About a year and a half after our high school graduation, the United States was suddenly in World War II. Some months later, my husband, Olan, was in Navy Officer Indoctrination at Ft. Skyler, New York, near New York City. I was in the city with friends. At the same time, Marie, who had become a WAVE in the navy was in training at Hunter College in New York. We spent one Sunday together seeing the sights of New York City. It was a beautiful spring day, and we rode on the top deck of a double-decker bus, went to the top of the Empire State Building, and then stopped at a restaurant where we ate lobster (and giggled as we used our nutcrackers and got all messy!) We felt a long way from Falfurrias where we had first become best friends.

*Lackey Cousins*

# VISITORS

Company was coming! Our out-of-town friends and family loved to visit us in South Texas. When they came, my sister Catherine and I went to the sleeping porch, and the company got our cozy pink bedroom. The sleeping porch was only partially glassed in and could be cold in winter, so we slept with hot water bottles and piles of covers.

Uncle Sam, my father's brother, and his wife, Gertrude, came from their home in Houston during the early part of dove hunting season each year. My father had access to lots of hunting locations because he knew the landowners well. Their take of birds was the limit nearly every hunt. Mother then made a tasty meal of fried dove (or quail). She made cream gravy to go with the birds that was most delicious, especially on homemade biscuits. For some reason, a meal of birds also called for Waldorf salad made with apples and celery.

Later in the hunting season, Uncle Charlie and Aunt Nell came from their home in San Antonio. They weren't related to us, but Mother and Aunt Nell felt like sisters. They had been dear friends when they were young girls in San Antonio and had stayed close. In the evenings at our house, there were lively canasta games with Charlie and Nell. They lived in a big house full of antiques and no children. Aunt Nell played "the horses" and bought antiques with her winnings. When she lost, she sold antiques. So there were frequent changes in the decor inside their home. Aunt Nell was a large person, but Uncle Charlie called her "baby" and showed only amusement regarding her gambling inclinations.

When folks from my father's side of the family came, they visited Auntie (Drusilla Myrick), my father's sister, too, while they were in Falfurrias. Our two families gathered for meals together. We heard stories about the days in Parker County (near Ft. Worth, Texas) where my father and Auntie had lived with their family. My father and Auntie exchanged childhood memories, often about cousins, aunts, and uncles. Auntie liked to remember how she chased the schoolteacher with a broom when she thought he unfairly punished one of her brothers. The teacher left town and never returned.

When we ate at Auntie and Uncle Joe's home, we always heard some of Uncle Joe's stories as we sat at the table. He liked to tell about the time he worked on building a railroad in Montclova, Mexico, and ate at the "Chinaman's" restaurant. The Chinaman served on black tablecloths unless a person wanted to pay a nickel extra for a white tablecloth. The restaurant was a gathering place for the railroad workers. Uncle Joe liked to tell the story about one worker who wrote on the Chinaman's wall:

> *Mexico, Mexico I do I do,*
> *I may die in hell,*
> *But never in you*

The fellow left Mexico but came back some weeks later and wrote on the wall:

> *Mexico, Mexico I do I do*
> *I'm not gonna stay*
> *I'm just passing through*

During the summertime, families with children came to visit—including cousins, distant cousins, and friends of cousins. The children liked to be shown around the farm. First, we showed them the tank and the water creatures—the turtles and frogs that leaped or slid into the water as we came up to them. Sometimes we threw bread into the water and watched the turtles fight for it. If we were lucky, we might see a wild mother duck swimming with a string of baby ducks behind her.

Next we stopped at the chicken house to check the nests for eggs. There was a lot of fluttering and protesting from the chickens, so we took only a few eggs and sometimes put them right back in the nests to gather later in the day.

Since the haystack was nearby, everyone had to climb up and slide (or jump) down—many times. And then we visited the cow lot. If there were small calves in a pen, some of the children tried to ride them. It rarely worked, but it was fun to try. If there was a bull on the farm, we went outside prepared with a red bandana or something else red. South Texas children were convinced that the color red made bulls furious and they would charge at it. Our bulls ignored us, but we did make sure we had a fence between us and the bull. We kept hoping we could make the bull angry enough to rush toward us.

If our horse, Fanny, was in the cow lot, we patted her and told her she was beautiful. And we usually found some fresh green grass to feed her. At times, she was saddled, and the children took turns riding—riding double.

For as long as Julian Palacios was our farm helper, our farm tour included a trip to his and his wife Cristela's little house. There was often a cute new fat baby at their house. At every visit, I asked Cristela to show us the christening dress her babies had worn. She kept it in a chest. It was long and so beautiful with lace, ruffles, and embroidery. Cristela and Julian eventually had seventeen children and most of them graduated from college Sometimes she cooked tortillas outside on a metal plate over an open fire. Then she gave each of us a tortilla.

Then we stopped at our garage. It had a dirt floor that had become quite sandy. It was the perfect place to find doodlebugs. They liked the soft, loose sand, and we found them in their little cone-shaped homes. We stirred the little cones with twigs and said, "Doodlebug, doodlebug, your house is burning down." The tiny bugs would soon appear. We put them in jars and then found a red ant bed and emptied the jars. We had heard they liked to eat ants. We didn't question the fact that the ants were much bigger than the doodlebugs.

We often stopped at the cattle water trough to look at the goldfish. We fed them bits of bread or tortilla and tried to decide if they were getting bigger.

Trees on the farm invited climbing. Some were quite easy with low branches, and others could easily take children to the top of the house—but those were discouraged. Sometimes a boy shimmied up the trunk of one of the big pecan trees and then kept climbing until the branches were small and he was swaying and bouncing. He would then call out to us below. We would tell him to come down. But he had gotten our attention!

In the heat of the day or if it was raining, we played board games and card games on the screened porch. One of the card games was called "Lindy," the nickname of Charles Lindberg, the aviator who first flew solo across the Atlantic Ocean. The object of the game was to make a successful trip by drawing cards that said "Gasoline, Fair winds, Smooth flying, Motor humming," and such. We sometimes played jacks on the screened porch. For a quieter time, we read the Bobbsey Twin books.

After supper in the cool of the evening, older folks gathered in chairs on the front lawn. We children still had enough energy to try cartwheels, backbends, and flips on the grass. If adults weren't too absorbed in conversation, they looked up to voice caution or give us applause.

Finally it was time for supervised baths. The bathtub could hold at least two or three little children at a time. Beds were pallets on the living room floor.

# MORE VISITORS

My Thomas grandparents and their children were the only ones in their large families who had ventured down into the South Texas brush country. There were lots of cousins back in Parker and Tarrant Counties in North Texas that my father and his sister, Auntie, spoke of often. They had been close friends with their cousins before coming to South Texas. Grandmother Thomas had been a Woody. Auntie and Ethel Woody were cousins and close in age. They had spent time together back in Parker County when they were young girls.

We had heard stories about Ethel. She was said to be very attractive and always quite conscious of her appearance. As a young girl, Auntie helped her mother with the four younger brothers in the family. There were lots of diapers to be washed. When Ethel Woody came to visit, Auntie told her that washing diapers made hands white and pretty, so Ethel pitched in, eager to help.

When I was quite young, word came that Ethel, her husband, and her two brothers were going to the Rio Grande Valley and would be stopping in Falfurrias for a visit. Ethel's two brothers had been mentioned by my family as the Woody boys who were New York lawyers. My grandparents and Auntie came to our house so we could all visit together when the Woodys came. I was anxious to see the people who were so special according to the adult conversations. Grandmother, with her long full skirt, had been asked to sit in the chair with the worn upholstery. At her advanced age, she would not be expected to stand up.

When they arrived, Ethel had on a hat, gloves, and a fur coat (it was winter.) I had never seen a fur coat before—it was beautiful! I wanted to touch it. Ethel was beautiful too. The Woody boys and my father and grandfather talked and had some chuckles about the Parker County days.

Auntie and Ethel exchanged information about folks they both knew. Then suddenly Ethel's husband stood up, and immediately the other visitors stood up, too. It was a signal that the visit was over. I managed to walk around the grown people and get close to the front door—and I touched the fur coat! It was so soft and smooth, much like the feel of Fluffy. Their visit was short; it wasn't like a South Texas visit with folks sitting for long leisurely conversations.

Some of the most intriguing out-of-town people were those who came to visit Uncle Joe and Auntie Myrick. Uncle Joe's mother was a pretty lady and said to be quite old when she first went down to South Texas from her home in San Antonio. She was probably in her eighties (she lived on into her late nineties). She had grown up in England, was an accomplished organist, and had played the organ for a huge Anglican church in Liverpool. Her speech was like that of an aristocratic English lady, and she looked so very dignified. She wore dark dresses with white lace collars, and her white hair was full and pulled into a bun. It was obvious that she was very devoted to Joe, her eldest son. It was not so obvious that she liked the place he had chosen to live, a little town so removed from any city.

Marvel was Uncle Joe's youngest sister. She was a strong presence when she came to visit. She talked about how exciting her life had been when she lived in California and knew movie stars. She was twice divorced. Our family often went to visit Auntie and Uncle Joe in the evenings. If Marvel was there, we asked her to sing for us. She had a magnificent singing voice. When she sang "Indian Love Call" with her strong rich voice streaming into the dark as we sat on Auntie and Uncle Joe's open porch, the plaintive song and her beautiful voice cast a spell that lingered in our memories.

Marvel's daughter, Emily, was in her late teens when she used to come to visit. She, too, told us startling stories about her life. One of her recollections was that of being kidnapped by her father. He kidnapped her in Texas and drove day and night as fast as he possibly could to California. She, too, met movie stars and saw the wonders of California. Finally she was sent back to her mother in San Antonio. She talked about having lots of boyfriends and how each one had asked her to marry him. I was much younger and thought she must have some unique special charm. I asked her, "How do you get a boy to ask you to marry him?" Her reply was, "You make him want to kiss you, but you don't let him." Okay, so good posture and a smile was not enough.

*Auntie (Drusilla Myrick)*

# AUNTIE

The best weekends for me were those visiting Auntie. In my young years, after school on Friday, my father often took me to her and Uncle Joe's home, and I stayed until Saturday evening. I experienced new things there, including learning how to make a pie and doing embroidery. I loved exploring the wooded pasture, the tank with scary snakes, and the dairy barn where we would watch the cows rush into their stalls, anxious to be milked.

At milking time in the dairy barn, the sweet smell of fresh milk mixed with the smell of cow feed and the excrement we were careful not to step in. I tried to milk a cow more than once but decided a special touch was needed. I did not have the touch. I liked looking into the separator house, especially if it was being used. The separator was a shoulder-high device with a large round container on top where the milk was poured in. A big handle on the side was turned by hand. Cream then came out of one spout and milk out of another spout. Each flowed into a separate container. The separator house was sparkling clean. After every use, Auntie scrubbed each of the separator's multiple parts, and the concrete floor was washed down daily.

Close to the barn, a tall silo was filled once a year with ensilage (shredded particles of grain and grain stalks). A machine sucked up the stalks from a truck, chopped them, and then reached to the top of the silo to blow the ensilage in. Through an opening in the bottom of the silo, cow feed was shoveled out to feed the cows. A delightful freshly-cut grass smell came from the silo.

Auntie and I went out to the big chicken yard full of Winedot chickens. We gathered the eggs and fed the chickens and checked their water. There was a rooster named Bobby that ran to us and stayed close by Auntie.

When she said, "Crow, Bobby," he threw his head high and his chest out to crow as loud as he could. Then we praised him with "Good boy, Bobby," and threw feed toward him.

Inside the house, I especially loved looking in Auntie's cedar chest. She had a peacock feather in there that was so delicate and soft. I stroked it and waved it in the air like a wand to see it swing and ripple. Peacock blue became my favorite color. There was a scarf in the chest that I liked to drape around me, feeling how soft and fuzzy it was. It was black with a tan edge around it. I thought it was fur, but it was actually a very plush velvet. And then there was the button box in the cedar chest. It had buttons with carvings and designs and different shapes—some shining and sparkling. Everything inside the chest had the lovely smell of cedar.

On Saturdays, we did some baking. Usually we made apple pies and sometimes others with meringue. I tried to make my smaller pie exactly like Auntie's larger one. In season, we gathered vegetables from the garden. There were green beans, peas, tomatoes, squash, and okra. I especially liked to gather asparagus, hear it snap as I broke it off, and then nibble the bright green tips.

Sometimes we walked to Los Olmos Creek nearby and went to the magical place with the moss tree. Once we dug clay from the creek bank, took it to Auntie's house, and shaped it into little cups and saucers. Then we baked them in the oven.

Sometimes, she showed me how to do embroidery and cross-stitch. If she was sewing a dress or piecing a quilt, she let me help—and even use the sewing machine after she showed me how to thread it.

At night when we were lying in bed, Auntie told me stories about the family history and about her life. She said that in 1882, at the age of six weeks, she made the journey to the Washington Territory with her parents and an older brother and sister. They traveled by train from Ft. Worth, Texas, to San Francisco, California, and then by ship to Bellingham, Washington. From there they went to Linden, which is close to the Canadian border.

The family was in the Washington Territory close to Linden for nine years, and Auntie had sharp memories of their time in the dense forests and their pair of oxen that pulled the wagon taking the family to town and taking the children to school and church. She remembered her pet pig Soloman that died in the forest fire that destroyed their home. She talked about her little brother who died of pneumonia. Shortly before his death, in a darkened room, he said, "Look! Pretty light." The family interpreted it as a vision of heaven. My grandfather, Henry, who had never been very religious, became deeply convinced of the heaven that the Christian Bible promises to believers. As a devoted Christian, he became quite a Bible scholar.

After the years in the Northwest, the family came back to Texas and lived in Weatherford, Texas, in Parker County. They raised cattle there until they came to Falfurrias in 1907. Sally, the older sister, was a quiet and compliant daughter—a real pleasure to her parents. Later, they approved of her marriage. Her parents found Auntie's high spirits tiring and irritating. They thought her friends should be only from the Baptist congregation, but she had friends outside the church. She was drawn to people she found interesting and entertaining.

My Grandmother Thomas, Auntie's mother, was a Woody before she married. And her mother was a Farmer. Parker County had several families with those names. They had all come from Tennessee. The Woody grandparents were said to have taken six months, walking most of the way to Texas and bringing with them only a shotgun, skillet, bedroll, and a hound dog. The hardworking and genial Woodys became prosperous landowners in Parker County. The Thomas families came from Tennessee by way of a Louisiana sugar cane plantation. One Thomas became a judge in Dallas, and another, Great-grandfather Isaac Thomas, was a judge in Tarrant County. Great-grandfather Isaac Thomas died when my grandfather was two years. His wife managed the ranch herself after her older sons left to fight in the Civil War—some for the north and some for the south. Auntie said her Grandmother Thomas smoked a corncob pipe. Sam Woody, an uncle, had a fleet of wagons that he used to transport freight for businesses and individuals. He was said to be a generous, congenial, and jovial man to travel with; "Around his campfire, the food was hearty and the bottle was passed around freely."

He is credited with changing the Tarrant County Seat from Birdville to Ft. Worth. He supplied enough liquor to folks working at the voting polls that they didn't realize some of the voters Sam brought in late were from outside the county. The voters who were brought in voted to move the county seat. The change barely passed. The county seat case was taken before the Supreme Court of Texas, and the decision was that Ft. Worth would become the county seat of Tarrant County.

Auntie talked about her younger life. At seventeen, she ran away from home and married Bailey Sanderfer. He was charming, good looking, and as high spirited as she was. She found him fascinating and appealing. His family was well educated and highly respected. His brother was the first president of Hardin-Simmons College and remained president for more than two decades. Bailey and Auntie went to the Northwest where Bailey worked for the Electric Power Company. They moved from place to place as electric power was being supplied to new communities. Life was good and full of new discoveries. Bailey was sent to San Francisco after the 1906 earthquake, and Auntie remembered the people there living in tents and cooking outside in Golden Gate Park.

She told of having a long stay in the hospital with a ruptured appendix while in San Francisco. Bailey was working in another city. She was near death. She was packed with ice and spoon fed for days while her body fought the poison. During the illness, she dreamed of a long, narrow bridge over a deep gorge. She was told to cross the bridge. She said she couldn't— she was afraid the bridge would not hold her. She was told she must get to the other side and that the bridge was the only way. She started to cross, but it was so frightening and so difficult and such a struggle. She stopped. Then she was told she must get across and she must do it alone. She made the effort, and after swaying, clinging, and straining, she moved slowly and cautiously and finally made it to the other side. Soon after the dream, her fever came down and she slowly recovered. The dream stayed fresh in her memory all of her life and perhaps gave her strength at times when she needed it badly. Perhaps it helped her believe she could accomplish almost anything—and "do it alone."

The work separations took their toll—Bailey was unfaithful, and Auntie divorced him. She found she had strength and determination, and she could indeed "do it alone." In San Francisco, she worked in a milliner shop, designing and styling ladies' hats. She also became a "practical nurse."

During her first marriage, she made one trip to Falfurrias to visit her family. Her father had asked her to come. She would not ask her parents for help after her divorce; she was too independent for that. But the day her brother John called to ask her to come and be with Annie Mae when the new baby came, she realized she could be of help. She had missed the support and sharing of a family, and she loved John dearly. So she assisted in the birth of my sister, Catherine, and helped take care of her as a baby. She became our beloved "Auntie." After a while, Auntie was in demand as a nurse for other women in Falfurrias who were having babies.

She was later asked to take a job with the Falfurrias Mercantile. She became a clerk in ladies' wear and soon became the buyer. She was a pretty lady and always gave the impression of self-assurance and competence. She had a well-informed knowledge of clothing, and her costumers came to rely on her judgment. For material sold by the yard, she could tell costumers how it would fall, pleat, or gather—and its quality. For Auntie, quality was always the most important. All of her life, she tried to have as much quality as possible.

Auntie met Joe Myrick when he came into the Mercantile store. He was tall and blond with blue eyes, and he had a lively sense of humor and lots of charm. He was an appealing fellow, especially when on his horse, which he rode so well. He was very attentive and made life seem venturesome and fascinating. They married and then lived on Joe's dairy farm.

Auntie's energies turned to life on their farm. She and Elofio, the farm helper, put in a large garden. She raised chickens, worked the bees, made a pretty yard, and was the best cook we ever knew. She also sewed for my sister and me and upholstered furniture for herself and for others in the family. Her company dinners were legendary, especially the rich homemade ice cream made with an egg custard and heavy cream from the dairy.

During World War II, Uncle Joe was a night watchman at the recycling plant out from Falfurrias; he rode his horse "Ranchero" around the fenced complex. Auntie spent her nights alone at the farm, always with a machete (a wide, sharp-bladed chopping tool) under her bed. That made her feel safe, but she never slept much. She read until the late hours. Even when she was ninety-five years old, she refused sleeping pills because she did not want to get into the "habit."

She kept Uncle Joe well fed—and anyone else who was around. For breakfast, it was bacon (but not for Auntie who never ate pork) and fresh biscuits with lots of Falfurrias Butter (never margarine) and homemade molasses or honey. After Uncle Joe was without teeth, lunch was twice-ground round steak patties, vegetables, and apple pie. Friends and neighbors just happened to drop by at mealtime. And Auntie never turned down a "wetback" who came by; they left well fed, too. She kept the hound dog food in the big container on the back of the stove. It was cornmeal mush seasoned with bacon grease and food scraps.

In our late-night conversations, she told me about how in her teen years her parents disapproved of her exuberance and how they deplored her eloping. But it was Auntie, with the help of a faithful lady helper named Demincia, who cared for her parents in their final illnesses. She took care of them in her home, nursing them, nourishing them, and giving them devoted attention.

Uncle Joe died suddenly at age ninety-one. Auntie had bad vision by then and had given up driving. She never had children. My brother, sister, and I were like her children. We tried to persuade her to rent an apartment in Kingsville (my home) or in Falfurrias. She was eighty-eight years old but determined to sell her farm and move into town in Falfurrias. She knew the exact street she wanted to live on, and she wanted to build a brick home. We children finally agreed and then helped her plan a house just for her needs. She sold the farm and built the brick house and lived in it for seven enjoyable years before she moved to Austin and lived her last year with my sister, Catherine. While in town in Falfurrias, she had her groceries and medicines delivered. Even her doctor made house calls to see her.

Auntie lived her life convinced that the United States was the best place in the world—other countries weren't safe or sanitary or as honorable. She refused to cross the Rio Grande and go into Mexico. And before my husband and I went to Europe (she tried to discourage the trip), she gave us toilet seat covers to take along. I still have them unopened. They are a keep sake that are truly in character for Auntie. She was a real patriot and took offence at any criticism of the United States. She never forgave President Carter for "giving away the Panama Canal." She loved President Eisenhower. In her later years we used to say she was the only woman in her nineties with her own foreign policy. Her mind and memory never diminished. About two days before her death, I asked her to show me the Eastern Star handshake. She whispered, "It's a secret."

She never thought she was special, but for her nieces, nephew and friends she was a living example of accomplishment, generosity, sincere graciousness, strength, and devotion to her family.

*Man With Mule pulling one-row Plow*

# THE WAY IT WAS DONE

When a person dares to reach way back in a closet and high on the shelf, there are sure to be surprises and discoveries. One of the things I found was a very old calendar that showed pictures of cotton growing—the planting, gathering, and ginning like it was done back in earlier days. Seeing the picture of the man behind a one-row plow pulled by a mule brought back memories of my grandfather, Henry Thomas.

Henry Thomas lived with our family on our small acreage the last few years of his life. As a vigorous young man, he had ridden up the Chisholm Trail, felled huge trees on his land claim in the Washington Territory, and raised cattle and farmed in North Texas and later in Falfurrias. Way back in the closet, I found one of his books, *Truck Farming in the South*, that was published in 1888. He must have wanted to learn more about farming in deep South Texas. When he lived with us in his late years, even with his fading health, he laid out an extended garden and worked the entire plot (with a one-row plow pulled by a mule). He also spent time looking out for the livestock, especially his mules. Caring for the land, growing things, and caring for the work animals had been his life and love.

When he came to live with us, his team of mules came too. His team had pulled his plows and wagon for years, and it was one of them that pulled his little one-row plow as he cultivated the garden plot in his new home. I could hear my grandfather saying "Jee" for right turn and "Haw" for left turn as he called out directions to the mule. These were also the terms used for other draft animals—horses and oxen. From those terms came a saying regarding people who did not agree. "They just don't Jee-Haw" was the expression. In a short time, my grandfather had a bountiful, thriving garden. He grew beans, squash, lettuce, corn, peas, and melons. He even had a long row of berries called "young berries." He kept us well supplied with fresh vegetables. As a small child, I enjoyed picking the beans, the peas and and shucking the corn as well as running between the cornstalks.

My grandfather also used his team of mules to pull his wagon that had come with him to our farm. He never learned to drive a car. He and my grandmother had always gone to town in their wagon or buggy to do their grocery shopping and visit their friends.

Seeing the pictures of the mules, I remembered conversations from years ago. People who had experience with mules agreed that the mules were much more intelligent than horses or donkeys. They had more endurance, were extremely surefooted, and were less temperamental. It was said they sensed danger and could avoid it. Supposedly they never ran into a fence or fell into a chasm or ravine. And for some strange reason, they were said to be attracted to gray or spotted horses; they would gather close to them and could be led by them. Mules have great strength. The word mule comes from the Latin word for labor. A mule is a hybrid—a cross between a horse and a donkey, preferably with a horse as the mother. Most of them are born male, and they cannot reproduce. They have a reputation for being stubborn, but I have no memory of my grandfather having difficulties with his mules. Perhaps that was because of his gentle nature and the years they had worked together.

In my grandfather's *Chamber's Encyclopedia*, published in 1889, which I found way back in the closet, it says mules were highly valued in the Mediterranean area and much care was given to their breeding in Spain and Italy and France. It also said, "Kings rode on mules and they were yoked to their chariots."

# THAT NEIGHBOR BOY

In the twenty-first century, there would be a label for our neighbor boy. Maybe he was academically challenged, had attention deficit, or perhaps was some kind of genius. In the 1920s and 1930s, Freddie Word was thought to be "not very smart and hard to control." Freddie was my age and lived with his family in the home next to ours. He was cute with sandy hair, blue eyes, and sharp features in his small, lean body.

We started school at the same time. In the early grades, Freddie used his school tablet paper to make boats, hats, and airplanes instead of writing his work as his teacher instructed him to do. He got laughs from the other students as he tried to read our books upside down. On the playground, he liked to change the rules any time he was not winning. He always "got there first" or "had the ball." When a teacher or another adult scolded him, he often said, "I dooz as I pleases." Freddie was forever chattering and telling other people how something should be done.

Almost every afternoon after school, Freddie rushed over to our house to visit and play. He would run up the lane that led to our house, and the two of us would play outside and sometimes try to fish in our tank with poles—tree branches, twisted safety pins, and string that Freddie put together. We would also climb up on the garage and swing down on a rope that he had attached to a nearby tree. If we played checkers or card games (fish or battle), he cheated and we had big arguments. He always declared that whatever he did or had was the best—his horse, his dog, and even his sister. He said his tank was bigger, his oranges were sweeter, and his mother's cooking was better than my mother's. He looked for arguments and loved them.

He was good at catching lizards and horn toads. We put them in boxes, and he always took them home with him. I argued that they were mine because they were on our farm, but Freddie "dooz as he pleases."

After some years, Freddie found an interest in electricity. He rigged a metal plate that he said took fingerprints. If a person put their finger on the plate, they were shocked. He made a radio and put battery-powered lights on wagons and old cars. He made a boat to use on the Word tank, and he worked on old castaway cars and got them to run again.

Somewhere along the way, he learned to read and write. One summer, he published a weekly neighborhood newspaper using a typewriter and a duplicating device. He gathered news and wrote the stories, had a gossip column and even ads. He charged five cents a copy when he sold them.

Another summer, he put together a two-wheel cart that had a curved, covered wagon top with a canvas over it. His horse pulled the cart with a harness that Freddie rigged. He wanted to drive the cart in the Falfurrias July Fourth parade, and he wanted Marie Bennett and me to ride in the cart with him. He hung a lantern on one side and a washtub on the other. Marie put on a baby-type bonnet with ruffles and stuck her head out of the canvas cover at the back of the cart. I sat in the driver's seat with Freddie and wore a long dress and bonnet. Freddie tried to look like an old pioneer with a broad-brimmed hat and red kerchief. About halfway through the parade, the rim of one of the wheels started coming off, and we started rolling along partially on the spokes of the wheel. Freddie pulled over to one side, took out a rope he had in the cart, laced it between the spokes and onto the rim and axle. We then pulled back into the parade and rode to the finish.

It seemed that Freddie could take any old car and make it run. He took me on trial runs in the makeshift vehicles, and we always got back home, but often he had to get out and tinker with something along the way.

Sometime during high school, Freddie went away to school in San Marcos. Afterward, we went in different directions. The word is that Freddie is gone now. And I wonder if he lived out his life with his mantra from long ago, "I dooz as I pleases."

*Mertie Jackson, Lucille Thomas, Sue Farr on top of Brooks County Courthouse*

# TOWN FRIENDS

When I visited my town friends, we wandered and explored their neighborhoods. Each home offered different places to explore and different people to visit.

When I visited my friend Marie Bennett, we always went to see her little grandmother who lived across the street. Her grandmother's yard was full of trees and vegetation, and the big, wide front porch had potted plants, hanging plants, and a porch swing. The shaded area was cool, calm, and peaceful. We usually had Grandmother Bennett's cookies for a treat.

Often Marie and I stopped to say hello to the Barnes family who lived in one of the few brick houses in town. And there was Miss Molly who was an older single lady who lived in a tiny doll-like house. Inside, she had pretty ruffled curtains and colorful beds and pillows, and the furniture and floors always looked bright and shiny. She loved company.

We also dropped in on Miss Majorie Sparks, our third-grade teacher. One day during class, she started coughing and could not stop. She left the classroom and never returned. We visited her at her home and told her we hoped she could come back to be our teacher. She lived only a short time after we saw her.

Marie and I were fascinated with the Catholic church. I went with my family to the Baptist church, and Marie went to the Presbyterian church. The Catholic church seemed quite different. We loved going to the open door of the entrance. The statues were intriguing, the altar was always decorated with flowers, and the stained glass windows were like jewels. I loved the scent and soft glow of the burning candles, and we saw people kneeling in prayer in front of the candles. We both wished our churches were that beautiful.

Skippy Ballard was another of my town friends. Her father was sheriff at the time, and she and her family lived on the bottom floor of the jail. There were prisoners in the jail upstairs. We weren't allowed to go up there, but Skippy showed me the stairs that led up to the second floor. In their boredom, the prisoners often looked down on the yard below where we played. They called out and liked for us to talk to them. Most of our replies were remarks telling them how bad they were. The prisoners then laughed; they were only amused.

I also spent time with Inez Sterling. Her father was a tall, handsome Texas Ranger. Falfurrias folks were glad to have him in their town. It made them feel safer. He was out on assignments often, but when he was at home, Inez and her friends were especially quiet because he was usually asleep. I remember seeing him on his living room sofa, stretched out and asleep with his boots and his hat pulled down over his face. From Inez's house, we could easily go to the high school grounds and skate on the sidewalks, or we could play on the seesaw and swings in the school superintendent's yard nearby.

The Wright sisters were fun to be with. Three of them—Nell, Jeanie, and Margaret—were near my age, and the four of us were twirlers in the band. Their house was full of laughs and teasing and lots of people—there were five daughters and one son.

Little Falfurrias became even livelier when the Jackson family moved to town. They had four children, and two of the girls were near my age. The family lived in a big two-story house. The Jackson girls loved to have slumber parties, and one of our favorite things to do was to climb onto the roof of their house and try to get the attention of people driving by on Highway 281. The Jackson sisters planned slumber parties in the Girl Scout hut in our Pleasure Park where we could jump in and splash around in the pool any time during the night. Another escapade was when several of us climbed onto the roof of the courthouse by going through a small window in the upstairs ladies' restroom.

Somewhere along the way, Saturday picnics in the eucalyptus grove began. In the Falfurrias early days, Mr. Lasater had eucalyptus trees brought in, and a thick grove of the trees grew just west of town. When I was able to drive, I was part of a group of girls that spent most of the day in the shade of the big trees. We packed lunches and brought *True Love* magazines and a package of cigarettes to share. We were as naughty as we dared and knew how to be.

# RANCH VISITS—RINCON

Since my father was the South Texas representative for the Houston Agriculture Credit Corporation, he got to know the ranchers who had loans with the company. He made regular inspection trips to the ranches and knew the owners and their families well. Most of them came to consider my father as part of their family.

One of the ranches that he visited for inspections was "Rincon" in Starr County, owned by a family named Wetzel. They had two lovely and vivacious daughters about the ages of my sister and me, so sometimes my father took my mother, my sister Catherine, and me when he went to their ranch. Mr. and Mrs. Wetzel seemed delighted to have guests and served hearty, delicious meals that we ate in their spacious kitchen. Mr. Wetzel was a vigorous man in his fifties who had the rugged look of a rancher with his weathered skin and his legs curving outward and slightly bent from his hours in the saddle.

To get to the ranch, we drove south from Falfurrias on Highway 281 and finally turned west. After a few miles of improved road, we drove on a narrow unimproved road through mesquite trees, cactus and brush, and then into Rincon where the long road was even narrower and the brush even thicker. Then suddenly there loomed a huge, two-story L-shaped building with multiple doors, each opening onto a long, wide porch. It was the Wetzel's ranch house. The structure had been built as a hunting lodge. Years before the Wetzels came to Rincon, the lodge had been deserted. The Wetzels lived in only a small part of the structure; the rest of the lodge was empty. There were remnants of furniture and shades in some of the bedrooms, but the bathrooms had been stripped of their fixtures during the long abandonment. The dining room echoed with a vast emptiness.

When we explored the big building, we imagined ghosts from the past lingering there—hunters in their brush jackets sitting in rocking chairs on the porches, smoking cigars or pipes, and looking out over the mesquite and thorny brush with deer and javelinas wandering and feeding on the grasses. The hunters might watch the wild turkey meander slowly to the water trough to drink beside the big Brahma cattle. And inside there might be people sitting near the fireplace telling hunting stories about the deer with large and strangely shaped racks of horns—or the doves that flew by in waves or the big coveys of quail that were flushed. And perhaps they told stories about sightings of snakes, bobcats, and Mexican lions out in the brush.

To my sister and me, it seemed like a lonely place, especially when the wind whipped and howled along the long porches. But the Wetzels loved their ranch and its wilderness and found that living in the old lodge was an adventure. The closest town was Rio Grande City, and they drove there from the ranch every day to get the mail.

The large herd of big Brahma cattle was intriguing. They had been rounded up by the men on horseback and brought into the huge pen for inspection. I was especially interested in the enormous bull. Brahma bulls are said to be the fiercest of all breeds. The one in the pen and all the cattle seemed completely docile, standing motionless except for chewing their cuds. I remembered hearing about the "drovers" in earlier days that drove longhorn cattle up the trails. They walked their horses slowly as they rode close by the sleeping cattle at night and sang softly to keep them calm. Maybe the Wetzels and their cowboys were also slow and gentle in handling their cattle.

One evening at Rincon, as our family was getting ready to leave, one of the Wetzel dogs was barking with loud fury beside the back porch. With a flashlight, we saw a giant rattlesnake coiled and ready to strike. Mr. Wetzel shot it and then shook his head and said, "This one was bigger than usual."

The Wetzel daughters were Mabel Lou and Margaret. At that time, there was a handsome young Falfurrias man who was a game warden in South Texas. My father told him he should visit the Wetzels and meet their daughter, Mabel Lou. He took the suggestion and paid them a visit. The two were immediately attracted to each other. A few months later, Mabel Lou and Lloyd McCullar got married in our farm home living room in Falfurrias.

After the Wetzel parents were gone, Rincon was sold and divided, but Lloyd and Mabel Lou stayed nearby, still in Starr County. They lived in their beautiful, new, modern ranch home that their architect son designed. They had large picture windows, so they were still looking out on the deep South Texas brush land.

# RANCH VISITS—LAGUNA SECA

The Laguna Seca ranch had been in the Vela family for generations, and Reynaldo Vela had become the owner. He had a loan from the company my father represented. The ranch was south of Falfurrias in Hidalgo County.

Unlike most South Texas ranchers, Reynaldo rarely wore a hat. He was a gallant gentleman, so perhaps he thought he should remove his hat in the presence of ladies. He was a handsome man with a sturdy build. His shock of hair was jet black, and his face was ruddy. Reynaldo had never married, and his ranch was his love. He raised Santa Gertrudis cattle on the several thousand acres of Laguna Seca (dry lake) ranch. The big lake on his ranch that had once been dry most of the time filled with water. Some years before, a search for oil resulted in finding artesian water. Through a dugout trench from the well, a stream of water flowed over a waterfall and then found its way into the old lakebed. Beside the stream were banana trees and other tropical vegetation. Under some large mesquite trees close by, Reynaldo had a concrete picnic table, benches, and a barbeque pit. Later, he built an arbor over the picnic table and an arched concrete walkway over the stream. Eventually, Reynaldo constructed a little house nestled into the trees beside the stream.

Tall, tropical cane-like plants surrounded the lake, and Reynaldo called the plants "tules." He stocked the lake with fish, and he loved to show and share his creation. He invited my father to come down with his family and friends. We went on many occasions and found it a delightful hidden treasure. It was there that we learned my father could cook on an open fire and catch big fish. There were also bird-hunting trips down on the ranch, and the hunters never failed to get their limits.

After the little house was built, we sometimes spent the night there. When we slept on our sleeping pallets, we were almost wall-to-wall people.

The house had electricity, but the darkness outside without the lights was the blackest we had ever known. The millions of bright stars in the sky seemed so very close. Usually it was extremely quiet, with only the night noises of the water creatures and insects, and sometimes the coyotes yapping and howling. But one evening we heard music. We did not have a radio on, and Reynaldo's ranch house was far from the campsite and there were no homes nearby. The next day, we asked Reynaldo about the music. He said he had planted watermelons on one of his acreages nearby, and the music on the radio was to keep the coyotes from coming to the field and eating the melons. The mystery was solved.

We were cautioned to look out for snakes, so we mostly stayed in the cleared area. On one trip, my brother shot a huge rattlesnake before breakfast. It was making its way into the tules.

It was wild and isolated where Reynaldo had created a true oasis in the wilderness, and he generously let us experience it.

*Uncle Will and Aunt Sally Lackey*

# RANCH VISITS—LACKEY RANCH

After my high school graduation in 1940, my sister, Catherine, and I went to visit our Aunt Sally Lackey, our father's older sister, who lived with her husband, Will, on a small ranch in northern New Mexico. The ranch was near Arroyo Seco, quite close to Taos, New Mexico.

Aunt Sally and Uncle Will Lackey lived in Falfurrias from 1908 to 1923. Some crop failures had been discouraging, so Uncle Will scouted for new country. Northern New Mexico captivated him—the lush green countryside and being able to irrigate with the abundance of water flowing from the upper Rio Grande River. He and Sally loved the idyllic mountainous location and how the fertile land produced in abundance.

Catherine and I found them living a sparse and primitive life. Their adobe home could be cold even in the summer. They heated it with wood stoves, but not in the summertime. They used oil lamps for lighting, and their indoor plumbing was limited to water in the kitchen. To take a bath, they heated water on the stove and then poured it into a washtub.

Aunt Sally proudly brought out her "feather beds." She said they would keep us warm at night. She put them on top of the mattresses, and we found that we sank deep down in them and could barely move. We had to wrestle with the feather bed just to turn over.

The Lackey yard was filled with vegetation, including apple, cherry, and pear trees. We gathered the juicy, sweet cherries and luscious pears. We also enjoyed gathering strawberries, peas, beans, and green leafy vegetables from the garden. Catherine used the fresh rhubarb to make a most delicious pie. Aunt Sally had a blooming flower garden with asters, hollyhocks, huge daisies, and other plants unknown to us. Little irrigation ditches with constantly flowing water ran through their ranch.

For groceries, we took trips into Taos, which was just a small village in 1940. It had a town plaza with low buildings all around it. One was a plush hotel with fine dining, We did not dine there but we got to know the cute bellboy and he came out to visit the ranch several times. There were other business buildings, all made of adobe with covered porches and walkways. The Indian men (called Pueblo Indians) walked into Taos from their nearby reservation. They stood on the porches and leaned against the walls of the buildings, often wrapped in their blankets. They wore brown buckskin looking pants and tunic , white leather leggings, and moccasins. Their long black hair hung down their backs in braids. We never saw them sit or speak; they just stood and looked out onto the plaza. They were an intriguing mystery.

We were told that our brother John called Uncle Will "Uncle Work" when the Lackeys lived in Falfurrias. We came to understand why—he was always busy. He milked cows in the early morning and in the evening. He tended to irrigation, took care of his beef cattle, and worked on pens and fences. The pond on their property froze in the winter, and before the ice melted in the spring, Uncle Will cut blocks from the ice and put the blocks in the icehouse with straw to keep the blocks separated and insulated. In the summer, he brought the ice blocks in and put them in the icebox. When it was haying time, Uncle Will lifted the bales of alfalfa alongside the younger men. He also loaded and hauled his beef cattle to take them to be sold.

We had two grown cousins, Daisy and Beth, whose homes were nearby. Each had become a widow before they came to the Taos area to be near their parents. After teaching school some years, Daisy married "T" and moved onto his farm. Catherine and I spent part of our visit with each of the cousins. When we were with Daisy, it was haying time. That meant her husband, T, and about six of the neighbor men were at their farm cutting the alfalfa, baling it, and putting it into the barn. It also meant that Daisy fed the men at lunchtime. She got up early and started cooking. We helped some, but Daisy was a whirlwind. She did jobs so quickly. At noon, she served the men mounds of fried chicken. She had chosen the chickens from her flock that morning. She had rung their necks, hung them to bleed, dipped them in boiling water, plucked them clean, dressed them, cut them up, and fried them. She also served bowls of frijoles, boiled potatoes, green vegetables, biscuits, and gravy. For dessert, she made strawberry shortcake. Catherine and I picked the strawberries in the morning. The men attacked the food and ate with starved appetites. There was little conversation. After finishing the meal, the men went directly to the field to work again. For two days, they harvested at Daisy and T's farm. Each of the neighbors helped at each of the other neighbor's farm or ranch. The smell of the freshly mowed alfalfa in the clean cool mountain air was so delightful it was almost intoxicating

Beth had three cute little children. She had a man friend who was a farmer and also a mail carrier. If he was busy with the hay hands, Beth delivered the mail. She left her children with a friend or her mother, and Catherine and I rode with her to make deliveries in her open-air touring car. When rain showers left water and great washouts in the dirt roads, we splashed and bumped along as we delivered the mail. Beth, with her delightful lighthearted sense of humor, laughed and joked with the folks as she delivered their mail. She enjoyed the rainy days. After big rains, the roads were completely impassable, so the mail could not be delivered. On those days, Catherine and I rode horses to get our mail at the Arroyo Seco post office. Catherine was engaged to Bob Allan, and he wrote to her often. I had a boyfriend in Falfurrias who wrote every day and sent the letters airmail—special delivery. There was no special delivery in that part of New Mexico unless it was on a horse.

Beth talked about walking the short distance to her parent's home in winter to help her father milk the cows. She said she had tiny icicles on her eyelids by the time she got to their place.

Our relatives and other people we knew there worked so hard. We thought their lives were terribly difficult, but they all seemed to be energetic and cheerful. On Saturday nights, they played—but not Aunt Sally and Uncle Will. There was always a dance at the small community hall in Arroyo Seco. Two people played the country tunes—a fiddle player and a fellow playing a larger bass string instrument. Dancing was lively and rowdy with lots of stomping and an occasional big "Whoop!" Some fellows now and then swigged from a little bottle they carried in their boot. We were shocked, but we danced along anyway. Back in Falfurrias, country music wasn't popular with people we knew.

One weekend, we went even higher in the mountains for a picnic. On the way there, the narrow road wound through a dense forest with a great canopy of trees and little rushing, swirling streams with waterfalls. After the climb, we reached an open meadow with a sweeping view that seemed to overlook the whole world. We then spread out the food and enjoyed the feast we had brought along. Someone even brought a freezer of homemade ice cream.

Another weekend, Daisy took us to some hot springs. We went underground in a big cave-like area and walked into the water. Steam rose from the hot water. There was a choking feeling from the stench of the fumes, and the water was deep, over my shoulders. We just stood in the water for a long time. The water was supposed to be beneficial, but Catherine and I could hardly agree.

We began to feel trapped by the mountains surrounding us. The plan was to go home with Falfurrias friends, the Dales, who were vacationing in Kansas and would soon come to visit with the Lackeys. Our plan was to stay six weeks with the Lackeys, and we were counting the days. Bob Allan paid us a visit in Arroyo Seco, and we were thrilled.

Finally the Dales arrived. We knew we would be rescued. Before heading back to Texas, Mr. Dale took us to Colorado Springs to see some of its wonders. The Garden of the Gods was spectacular, and we had always heard of Pike's Peak—and there it was!

So we had had our visit to a small northern New Mexico ranch and our Lackey relatives. We were so happy to return to our family and little Falfurrias.

After some time, Catherine and I realized we had spent time with our dear and quite contented Lackey family and had a rare adventure and an inside look at a vanishing way of life. Even during their busy lives, they had entertained us and embraced us as family. Looking back, it was a time that I now cherish. My husband and I visited northern New Mexico many times in years that followed, and we loved it. Catherine and I were there before artists and tourists began flocking to the region, and we experienced its more primitive era. The Lackey home site is now part of the Taos Ski Resort.

# TEXAS A&I IN THE EARLY 1940S

In the fall of 1940, my parents took me to the Smith House in Kingsville so that I could live there while attending the college of Texas A&I (now Texas A&M University—Kingsville). They had known "Ma" Smith when she and her family had lived in our hometown of Falfurrias, and they thought I would be in good hands. My father gave me the following advice: "Take business courses; a good secretary can always get a job."

The Smith House was a white two-story house just two blocks from the campus. About twelve girls roomed and had their meals there. We freshmen wandered around and found our way to registration, the bookstore, and later to our classes. Among other discoveries, we found that many of the students streamed into the T Jack store when they had free time. The T Jack was across the street from the campus. It had food, drinks, class supplies, music from the nickelodeon, and lots of socializing (there was no student union building back then).

Students also clustered in the arcade between the two main buildings, Manning Hall and Neirman Hall. Between classes, they gathered to smoke (smoking was considered adult and safe back then) and to chat. The young lady students wore dresses or skirts with socks and oxford shoes. The young men wore dress shirts, dress shoes, and sometimes ties and coats. Some young men had slide rules hanging from their belts. That was impressive; it meant they took engineering, math, or science courses. The students shared their campus experiences, including what their classes were like and stories about their professors.

Several of my professors are especially memorable. I took a course from Miss Mamie Brown, an education teacher. In one of her class periods, each of the students was to give a brief presentation in whatever area he or she might be teaching. My roommate was an elementary education major and had lots of charts and mounted pictures to teach concepts. I borrowed her "number" pictures. When I got to four in my presentation, the picture was of four roses—Four Roses was the name of a Seagram's whiskey. Suddenly Miss Mamie sprang from her seat and told me to sit down. Apparently my presentation was in poor taste. During the same class, a male student—Dono Moore from Falfurrias—started his presentation of a biology lesson. He drew the evolutionary tree and started to label the branches. Again Miss Mamie jumped from her seat and told him to sit down and then erased the board. He had offended Miss Mamie; she was a fundamentalist with convictions, and there would be no mention of evolution in her class!

In my freshman year, Miss Edith Cousins was my English teacher. She was the daughter of Texas A&I's first president. She always seemed to have a troubled expression, as if she was burdened. Perhaps teaching students was part of her mission in life—yet a burden. She told us about the hardships of the students during the Depression and how some male students lived in the utility tunnels on campus while they attended college. She often told us how very privileged we were. She had lived in China and traveled widely. She had studied the major philosophies and found that they all had similar values; she found virtues in all of them. She tried hard to enlarge our world and surely did, but she also raised our compassion toward her. She never married and shared a home with her mother, a tiny woman who wore big hats and carried a huge horn to help her hear.

Another memorable professor was Dr. DeWitt Davis, a psychology teacher. He was a small, wiry man with a mustache. He, like his fellow professors, always wore a coat and tie to class (and this was before air conditioning.) The word was that Dr. Davis never graded his tests, that no one had to study for his multiple-choice exams, and that all his students made As and Bs. I heard the stories and unfortunately believed them; I have the D to prove it. He loved to use extrasensory perception cards in class. They were about the size of playing cards with symbols like circles, triangles, and wavy lines. He lifted a card from the deck, looked at it, and put it on a pile. We students were supposed to write down what we thought the symbol was. Dono "Ox" Moore, who sat on the front row of the classroom, did so well in naming the symbols that Dr. Davis became convinced that Dono was truly gifted with extrasensory perception. He wanted him to go to his office for more testing. Dono always said he had to go to football practice. Years later, Dono confessed to friends that Dr. Davis's desk was so shiny he could see the reflections of the symbols as Dr. Davis put the cards on the desk.

And there was Dean John E. Conner, our academic dean. (He was one of three deans; the others were dean of women and dean of students). Mr. Conner was also a history professor. When he taught American history, he told us his personal stories along the way. We learned about the cattle drives that came through the middle of the little West Texas town, Pontotoc, where he had lived. The children couldn't go to school because the cattle drive lasted all day, and the children could not cross the street to get to the school. He rarely got past the Civil War in his classes, but what he covered was so interesting! He knew his students very well, and he knew South Texas even better. He soon learned the names of the parents of the students and even the counties they were from, and then he asked about them when he met us in the halls. People often came to him with various objects to identify. Usually he knew what the items were and what they were used for—and if not, he would find out. He found life exciting and made it exciting for his students. Eventually he had accumulated so many objects that people had given to him that he needed a large place to put them. A building was cleared out to house the collection, and it came to be called the Conner Museum. Later, the collections were moved across the street to a new and larger Conner Museum. The large accumulation of South Texas memorabilia and displays now serve to teach out-of-town visitors, young children, and townspeople in the area. It is interesting to note that Dean John Conner published his last book, *A Great While Ago*, when he was one hundred years old. He died in 1989 at age 106.

In spite of my father's advice, I majored in history (after I took shorthand and typing.)

A person only has to drive by Texas A&M University—Kingsville to notice some of the changes. There are now many automobiles; in 1940, students walked everywhere, even to downtown, and they stayed in Kingsville most weekends. Students dress more casually now, and if you see a professor, he or she most likely will be dressed casually, too. Campus security people and vehicles are always visible. In 1940 and for years beyond, campus security consisted of one night watchman who checked to see if the doors to the buildings were locked in the evenings.

*Mary Lou Pena (standing) Mother Anita Esquivel (seated)*

# MARY LOU PENA REMEMBERS HER TEEN YEARS

At Melida's Beauty Salon in Kingsville, conversation flows in all directions. One day, someone said something about when cicadas begin their shrill serenade on summer evenings. Mary Lou Pena, a hair stylist at Melida's, commented that you could hear the cicadas singing when cotton pickers left the fields after sundown. She said she had spent part of her teenage summers picking cotton, and she remembered hearing them then.

When asked what it was like to pick cotton, Mary Lou said, "It was fun!" Then she told us about the days of working in the fields near Kingsville, Recardo, and Falfurrias at picking time. A fellow with a truck made arrangements with teenagers and others and then drove to their homes early in the mornings to get them. In Mary Lou's family (the Esquivels), there were seven children. Five of them were picked up very early in the morning to go work in the cotton fields.

All the workers had to wear clothing that completely covered them, including a large hat for protection from the sun. Gloves were necessary because of the sharp points of the cotton shell (or burr). Some farmers insisted on "clean cotton," which meant the cotton had to be picked from the shell. Other farmers allowed "pulling," so they gathered the complete cotton boll. They walked between two rows of cotton and pulled a long sack with a strap that went over the neck and shoulder. Their hands were free to reach out for the bolls. There was competition among the pickers, so friendly banter went back and forth—some bragging, but some also helping other pickers fill up their bags. The five Esquivel children had a goal—to gather a thousand pounds before lunch. They usually did it and always beat the competition!

At lunchtime, the hats and gloves came off, and the pickers ate their lunches reclining in the shade under the truck and cotton trailer. Mary

Lou said it was quite a large truck. Her mother, Anita Esquivel, packed lunches for her children to bring with them. Lunch was a social time for the teenagers with jokes, lots of teasing, and a little flirtation.

Then it was back to the fields for as long as there was daylight. Around 4:30 or 5:00, someone would start singing favorite Spanish songs and ballads and everybody else soon joined in. They sang till the end of their workday when they pulled their sacks to the truck to be weighed. The pay was between $1.25 and $1.50 per hundred pounds, depending on the decision of the fellow with the truck.

When asked what she did with her money, Mary Lou said she and her brothers and sisters gave all their money to their mother. Each of the children received money from their earnings for the Saturday afternoon movie at the Rialto Theater. They got to the theater when it opened and stayed until it was almost dark. They loved the air conditioning, and popcorn was just five cents a bag.

Some of their money was used to buy school clothes, and Anita gave each child a nickel every day to spend after school. They walked to and from school, and on the way home they stopped at a small store named Vidaurri's and bought a treat. Mary Lou's favorite was a little pink patty of candy with nuts.

People occasionally told the children that someday machines would pick cotton, but the children knew it was not true. Machines could never pick cotton like people could!

*Frank Graham and wife Joy*

# FRANK GRAHAM, RETIRED RANCH FOREMAN

After a visit with South Texas retired ranch foreman Frank (Pancho) Graham and his wife, Joy, it was easy to understand why Frank has been a consultant for TV documentaries about South Texas ranching. He has done presentations on ranch life, including rope making with the fibers of *lechuguilla*, a kind of cactus, and the Spanish dagger plant. He has lived the life of the ranch country and worked alongside the vaqueros for most of his life. Before retiring, he was foreman of three of the Jones's ranches west of Falfurrias. As foreman, he was responsible for all fences, water, feed, doctoring of the animals, and clearing land when necessary, He also took guests hunting and saw to it that the ranches made money along the way.

Frank grew up in Brownsville where he worked in his father's dairy. Spanish-speaking workers also worked in the dairy, so Frank grew up hearing both English and Spanish and was eventually completely bilingual. After Frank finished high school, he served two years in the U.S. Navy and married Joy. Frank worked in a laboratory as a gas analyst for Union Carbide and later Amoco before spending ten years with Amour & Co. In order to support three little children, Frank and Joy decided to extend their college education. They moved to Lubbock to attend Texas Tech. While there, Frank taught a class called Meat Cutting.

But for a more permanent job, Frank came back to South Texas to work as a cowboy on the Jones's ranches west of Falfurrias. He was asked to be the ranch foreman and to move his family to a house at the main ranch. He lived and worked on the Jones's ranches for more than thirty years. Joy taught school and always had long commutes to her jobs.

To see Frank is to realize he has been a man of the outdoors. The blistering Texas sun has left lines and freckles on his fair skin. His engaging smile shows stains on his teeth from the use of tobacco, like that of many ranchmen of his era. His dark brown eyes sparkle as he remembers the people he worked with and the amusing tales they exchanged. Ranchmen are rarely without their hats, and Frank's light colored felt hat with its traditional upward curves on the sides usually covers his thick silver hair.

Frank has the heart, soul, and understanding of a vaquero—recognizing the different temperaments of the horses and cattle, knowing the plants and terrain, and having the Spanish words that describe them so well. He talked of the long hours spent in the saddle at round up and branding time and going from one ranch to another on trails by horseback. There were no hard surface roads for cars on the ranches in the early years. The deep sand was impossible to drive an automobile through. The meals for the vaqueros were prepared in one or more of the line camps (a sort of shed) that sheltered only the cook who worked over a wood fire. There was water at the line camps but no electricity. Frank had high praise for the food that was prepared. He says he has had no beans as tasty as those he ate at the camps. Recently, he and Joy listed the full names of the vaqueros Frank worked with—from memory. There were ninety-six on the list. Considering Frank's deep respect and appreciation for the vaqueros, it's easy to see how he had their complete loyalty.

Frank is a student of South Texas history. He is able to recall owners of the various ranches for over a hundred years back. He also recalled some of the stories of eccentric ranch owners. Many of the owners were quite frugal and miserly, and one even considered canned peaches brought onto the ranch as much too frivolous. For another, serving syrup to the cowboys was forbidden—they would eat too much *pan de campo* (camp bread) if they had syrup!

The ranch owners could be crude. One rancher loved to chew bubble gum. When he ate, he saved the gum by putting it behind his ear. And there was a lady rancher who would never hire an Irishman unless he had been a Texas Ranger.

Older men in South Texas were often referred to as "Old Man." There is a story about "Old Man Bill Jones" visiting his neighbors and not wanting to take the long road around to the entrance. He cut the fences and drove his cart (pulled by mules) through. Some of his neighbors said he appeared as a visitor any time of day or night—and sometimes spent the night. When a guest in the Corpus Christi Nueces Hotel dining room asked the waiter to tell the old man at another table to stop slurping his soup, the waiter told him, "I can't. He's Mr. Bill Jones, and he owns this hotel."

There is also a story about Mrs. Henrietta King. When the railroad was being built across her King ranch land, she offered to pay the railroad workers five cents for every rattle taken from a rattlesnake that had been killed. Soon barrels were piled high. She decided to reduce the amount she would pay to three cents a rattle because she was spending too much money.

When Frank showed me his collection of books, I realized his wide knowledge of South Texas, its ranching, and the people who have been a part of the Texas heritage. One long row of books was only about horses. Again, it showed Frank's love of horses. There were Longhorn cattle books as well as impressive Longhorn paintings in his home. So it was not surprising to learn that he and Joy had a herd of them on part of one of the Jones's ranches, descendents of the famous Graves Peeler Longhorns.

Frank is retired now from actively ranching, but he and Joy found a South Texas home that seemed just right. The home is in the country, sits back from the road, and has a brown rustic appearance with a long porch across the front. The place has several tree-shaded acres including a grassy pasture.

Frank does not ride horses anymore since his three back surgeries, but he still keeps three beautiful horses that graze in the pasture in front of the house. He raised them and cared for them as he had cared for their mothers and grandmothers, and he plans to continue to care for them, too.

*Olan Kruse*

*John and Larry Kruse*

# LOOKING BACK—LOOKING AHEAD

Now, in 2010, Falfurrias is still in my life. My son, John Kruse, lives on the old Thomas farm in the home where his mother was born. He moved to Falfurrias after retiring from his work with two Texas agencies in Austin. The farm is smaller. It is now thirty-four acres, about the right size for John's horses and few beef cattle. His children, Chris and Jolana, and her husband, Omar, and their children, Amorie and Major, love to visit just as other grandchildren came in years past, including John himself. Since my home in Kingsville is only thirty-six miles from Falfurrias, it is easy to visit the farm. Some things have changed, but in my memory I can see it just as it used to be with the big pecan trees where the cypress tree now stands. I see the citrus orchard where the new garage was built. Now there is a big storage building instead of the little barn with stalls for the cows that were milked.

After my Falfurrias high school graduation in 1940, I spent two years as a student at Texas A&I College in Kingsville. It was there that I met Olan Kruse, a fellow student and my husband to be. Olan was a handsome fellow and great fun to be with. He had a sweet and appealing slightly crooked smile. He wore a slide rule on his belt that gave him an elite identity. He was a physics major.

World War II descended upon us in December 1941 and changed the direction of everyone's life. After his graduation in May 1942, Olan took a job that sent him to radar training with the Signal Corp in Belmar, New Jersey. We planned to be married in September 1942. Olan could not get leave to come back to Texas after so few months at his job. My father could not leave his work at that time either. So Olan's parents and I took the train to New Jersey for our wedding. For our honeymoon, we went to Atlantic City over Labor Day weekend. On the Million Dollar Pier, we saw Bud Abbott and Lou Costello perform, and we saw a horse jump from a high diving board into a tiny tank. A fortuneteller told us that Olan would go into the navy and we would have two sons. After the whirlwind honeymoon, we settled in for a cold winter in Belmar. I took a clerical job with the Signal Corps.

Olan wanted to enlist in the service, so he began investigating the different branches of the military. He was offered a commission in the navy and entrance into pre-radar school at Harvard and advanced radar at MIT. That was his choice.

The Navy first sent Olan to indoctrination at Ft. Skyler in New York for three months. I saw Olan on weekends since I lived in New York City while he was there and stayed with Eleanor Pfluger, a long-time acquaintance of Olan's from Bishop, Texas. Eleanor was in New York to be near her husband who was also in the military. We lived with her aunt and the aunt's husband, the Tupaks. The Tupaks had a restaurant in Queens that served only lunch, and they lived in the upstairs above the restaurant. Eleanor and I worked in the restaurant at rush hour. Many of the costumers were from a Revlon cosmetic plant that was nearby. They stormed in at lunchtime with their lipstick-smeared white coats, shoved each other for seats at the counter and tables, and then shouted their orders. Wow, these were the kind of people that gave New York a reputation of rudeness! I did learn how to make sandwiches in a hurry. "Aunt Minnie" Tupak and her husband were dear and generous people, and Aunt Minnie was an excellent cook. The restaurant was packed to capacity at lunchtime.

After being in New York, Olan and I moved to Cambridge, Massachusetts. Olan finished the Harvard and MIT radar courses and then he was asked to come back to Harvard to teach. At the end of each pre-radar class, we thought he would be ordered to duty on a ship. We were grateful for each renewed assignment that left him in the United States. While living in Cambridge, I worked in a lab at Polaroid where optical range finders were being processed. Later I worked at Radcliff University in the alumnae office. Olan continued to get orders to teach until the Harvard school closed, and then the Navy sent him to teach pre-radar at Bowdoin College in Brunswick, Maine. When the war ended, the Bowdoin radar school closed. Olan received orders to go to Hawaii. I came back to Falfurrias and had a baby—our first son, John. Olan had three weeks to explore Hawaii and then came back—and later came to me and our baby boy in Falfurrias.

Olan's plan was to use the GI Bill and do graduate work in physics at the University of Texas in Austin. The summer before he was to enter UT, he took a math course at Texas A&I in Kingsville. Discharged World War

II veterans were flooding the college campuses as they streamed in to use their GI Bill for education. More teachers were needed. Olan's professor asked him to stay on to teach one year. He accepted. Along with other new faculty and students, we lived in the vacated barracks of the Naval Air Station in Kingsville.

Olan entered graduate school in 1946. Again, he was asked to teach! He taught one or two classes each semester while he was a student. We spent five years in Austin and had our second son, James Lawrence (Larry), before moving to Nacogdoches, Texas, where Olan was chairman of the Physics Department and established a physics major at Stephen F. Austin College. The lush, scenic, and historic old town of Nacogdoches is centered in the deep piney woods of East Texas.

It was at Stephen F. Austin that I finally went back to college, first taking only one course at a time. It was also there that John started playing Little League baseball, and Olan was a coach for his team. We seemed entrenched in the little town of Nacogdoches. After much planning and selecting, we built a house. We lived in the house a few months before an offer came to Olan from Texas A&I, his alma mater in Kingsville. The offer was for chairman of physics. President Poteet also wanted him to plan a new physics building. The answer was no; we didn't want to leave our new home, Nacogdoches was a pleasant place to live, and Olan loved his work.

One year later, Texas A&I sent him the same offer. We always thought we would spend our retirement years in South Texas, back in home territory, but we weren't near retirement. However, we knew our boys loved visiting grandparents and relatives in Falfurrias. We would be close to them and to the other grandparents in Robstown. And we could lend help as our parents grew older. Okay! Olan accepted the offer. We had lived in Nacogdoches for five years.

We were back in South Texas again. I finally finished my degree in history, nineteen years after starting. I was asked to establish a second grade that was being added to the Epiphany Episcopal school. I accepted and taught for twelve years. Little League and Pony League baseball continued to be a big part of our lives as both of our sons played for a total of twelve years and Olan was assistant coach most of those years.

For our sons, hunting with their Grandfather Thomas and fishing with their Grandfather Kruse gave them great shared experiences and adventures. There were visits with my parents and Auntie and Uncle Joe in Falfurrias. They loved to hear Unvle Joe's stories. I loved seeing our boys explore the Falfurrias farm, ride the horse, and hunt there with their BB guns. And the little Falfurrias farm stayed a part of our lives. After my parents were gone, Olan and I had it by ourselves for seventeen years. We called it our "work farm." We went over on weekends to mow, water, work on fences, saw the trees after the freezes, and just sit on the patio, sip a cool drink, and watch the birds. We had parties at the farm, and friends came over from Kingsville. I always insisted that the guests take a walk out to the tank to see the water creatures and any unusual birds that might be visiting.

According to the signs on the highways, Falfurrias now has a population of 5,296. There are still businesses on the main street (Rice Street), including a big new Whataburger. There is a highway 281 north-south bypass. More businesses are on the old 281 Highway, including an HEB grocery store, a new bank, a new school (not as attractive as the one before), inviting rustic restaurants, motels, and a Wal-Mart! The dairy business is gone, but butter is still being made in Texas that bears the Falfurrias Butter name. More and more of the population is Hispanic. Prized recognition has come to the high school, including the mariachi musical group, the baseball and track teams, as well as the drama productions. The school recently received a national award for their historical presentation, Hernandez vs. Texas, the Supreme Court case that solidified that a person must be tried by a jury of his or her peers.

The railroad no longer passes through town, and in fact, the rails have been removed. But the big eighteen-wheeler trucks speed up and down Highway 281 night and day. This is NAFTA! Falfurrias has four traffic lights, and it is in the process of getting five overpasses so the trucks can move even faster!

The nearby big ranches are an attraction for birders, photographers, and hunters. Folks drive or fly in to hunt deer, doves, quail, and exotic game or just to visit the vast acres of wilderness brush country.

The farm now has city water. More streets and country roads have been paved and named. The farm now has an address on Travis Road.

Much of the time, folks in the little town of Falfurrias and its brush country still pray for rain, and when it does come, life is renewed—the desert is revived, and the land blossoms once again.

*Thomas Farm Home*

*"I cannot but remember such things were, that were most precious to me."*

—*William Shakespeare*